Contents

What Is a Noun?

A **noun** is a word that names a **person**, **place**, or **thing**.

1. Circle the nouns that name a **person**.

   Tom run girl pretty man Maria grandfather hide doctor

2. Circle the nouns that name a **place**.

   school library small backyard eat falling mall beach Michigan

3. Circle the nouns that name a **thing**.

   ask lamp pencil walking tell grow coat car tree

4. Circle all the **nouns** in each group of words. Remember that a noun names a **person, place,** or **thing**.

   a) shoe   sing   carrot   basement   quickly

   b) big   teacher   cried   bed   soft

   c) baby   wanted   sister   strong   bedroom

5. Circle the **nouns** in each sentence.

   a) The kitchen is very clean.

   b) Carlos ran quickly down the street.

   c) The truck drove past our house.

   d) Mom painted the bathroom.

6. Write a sentence that has three nouns.

   ____

7. Write a sentence that includes a person and a place.

   ____

8. Write a sentence that includes a person, a place, and a thing.

   ____

© Chalkboard Publishing

Cut out pictures from magazines and fliers that represent nouns, and paste them below.

What Are Proper Nouns?

Nouns that always begin with a capital letter are called **proper nouns**. The following kinds of nouns always begin with a capital letter:

Specific places, such as a **country, state, city,** or **town.**
Examples: United States, California, Houston

Names of **holidays.**
Example: Labor Day

Names of **people** or **pets.**
Examples: Mr. Brown, Dr. Chong, Fluffy

Names of **days of the week** and **months of the year.**
Examples: Monday, June

1. Use a proper noun to complete each sentence.

   a) I would like to visit the state of ____.

   b) The first day in January is ____.

   c) Little Rock and _____________________ are American cities.

   d) _________________________________ was my teacher in Grade 2.

   e) My favorite day of the week is ____.

2. Write eight proper nouns.

   _________________________________   _________________________________

   _________________________________   _________________________________

   _________________________________   _________________________________

   _________________________________   _________________________________

Remember to check your writing for proper nouns. Did you use capital letters for all proper nouns?

© Chalkboard Publishing

Making Nouns Plural

To make many **nouns** plural, just add the letter **s**.

Examples: rock – rocks   window – windows   flower – flowers

For some nouns, you need to do something different. Watch for nouns like the ones below.

Nouns ending with…	To make the noun plural…
s, **x**, **ch**, or **sh**	Add **es** *Example: one fox – two foxes*
consonant + **y**	Change the **y** to **i** and add **es** *Example: one fly — two flies*

1. Use **plurals** of the **nouns** below to complete the sentences. Use each noun only once. Choose a noun that makes sense in each sentence.

   wish   dish   match   bunny   box   bush

   a) After dinner, I helped wash the _______________________.

   b) I saw two _______________________ in the park today.

   c) My mother planted two _______________________ in the backyard.

   d) Pablo packed his books into two _______________________.

   e) In the fairy tale, the girl got to make three _______________________.

   f) Dad used _______________________ to light the candles on the cake.

2. Rewrite each sentence to make the underlined nouns **plural**. **Do not** use the words **a** or **an** before a plural noun.

   a) I got a <u>scratch</u> on my <u>arm</u>.

   ____

   b) I saw a <u>lady</u> wearing a <u>dress</u>.

   ____

Tricky Plural Nouns

Making some nouns plural is tricky!
Be careful when making plurals from nouns that end with the letter **o**.
For some nouns that end with **o**, add the letters **es**.
For other nouns that end with **o**, just add the letter **s**.

Add *es*	Add *s*	
echo – echoes hero – heroes potato – potatoes tomato – tomatoes	patio – patios photo – photos piano – pianos radio – radios	video – videos zero – zeros

1. Complete each sentence below by writing a **plural noun** from the lists above.

    Choose a word that makes sense in the sentence.

    a) The restaurant has two _________________ where people eat outside.

    b) There are two _________________ in the number 100.

    c) We picked the _________________ that were red and ripe.

    d) All _________________ have black keys and white keys.

2. Rewrite each sentence below to make the underlined nouns **plural**. **Do not** use the words *a* or *an* before a plural noun.

    a) The <u>hero</u> turned on a <u>radio</u> to hear the news.

    ____

    b) Larry sent me a <u>photo</u> of a <u>potato</u> from his garden.

    ____

    c) In the <u>video</u>, people heard an <u>echo</u>.

    ____

© Chalkboard Publishing

Tricky Plural Nouns (continued)

Watch out when making plurals from nouns that end with the letter **f**.
For most nouns that end with **f**, change the **f** to a **v** and add **es**.
For a few nouns that end with **f**, just add the letter **s**.

Change *f* to *v* and add *es*		Just add *s*
elf – elves	shelf – shelves	chef – chefs
half – halves	thief – thieves	cliff – cliffs
leaf – leaves	wolf – wolves	roof – roofs
loaf – loaves		sheriff – sheriffs

3. Complete the sentences below by writing a **plural noun** from the lists above. Choose
   a word that makes sense in each sentence.

   a) You can share an apple by cutting it into two ___________________.

   b) The ___________________ stole many bicycles.

   c) Three ___________________ howled loudly during the night.

   d) The library has many ___________________ full of books.

4. Rewrite each sentence to make the underlined nouns **plural**. **Do not** use the words
   a or *an* before a plural noun.

   a) The <u>chef</u> made a <u>loaf</u> of bread.

   ____

   b) A <u>leaf</u> blew onto the <u>roof</u>.

   ____

   c) It is dangerous to play near a <u>cliff</u>.

   ____

   d) The <u>sheriff</u> caught a <u>thief</u>.

   ____

© Chalkboard Publishing

Tricky Plural Nouns (continued)

Do not be tricked by tricky **plural nouns**!

For nouns ending with the letters *fe*, change the *f* to a *v* and add *s*.
Examples: knife – knives   life – lives   wife – wives

To make these nouns plural, do not change anything!
Examples: one fish – two fish   one sheep – six sheep   one deer – four deer

You will need to remember the tricky plurals below.

Singular	Plural
child	children
foot	feet
goose	geese

Singular	Plural
mouse	mice
person	people
tooth	teeth

5. Complete each sentence by writing a **plural noun** from the lists above.

    a) My father uses _________________________ to cut vegetables for dinner.

    b) When we went fishing, my sister caught three _________________.

    c) I like to learn about the _______________ of famous people.

    d) The three woolly _________________ ran away.

6. Rewrite these sentences to make the underlined nouns **plural**. **Do not** use the words *a* or *an* before a plural noun.

    a) The <u>wife</u> made lots of food for the party.

    ____

    b) A <u>mouse</u> ran over my <u>foot</u>!

    ____

    c) The <u>child</u> fed the <u>goose</u>.

    ____

    d) The <u>woman</u> saw a <u>deer</u> in the woods.

    ____

© Chalkboard Publishing

Nouns Review Quiz

1. Complete the sentences about **nouns**.

    a) A noun can name a ________________, ________________, or ________________.

    b) A ____________ noun is a noun that always begins with a capital letter.

2. Underline all the **nouns** in each sentence.

    a) Mom put your mittens on the top shelf in the closet.

    b) Bees and butterflies visit the flowers in our backyard.

    c) The mountains in Colorado are amazing to see!

    d) The nurse gave the doctor some papers to read.

    e) If the windows are closed, how did a bird get in the house?

    f) Darnell went to the beach with some friends.

3. Change the first letter in **proper nouns** to a capital letter.

    a) I saw mrs. greenway at the mall last tuesday.

    b) My dog rover is coming to maine with us.

    c) Will dr. conway come to dinner on thanksgiving?

    d) Is chicago one of the largest cities in the united states?

    e) I think uncle alfred will spend the winter in florida.

    f) Every year, valentine's day is on february 14.

4. Write the **plural** of each noun.

a) box _______________ b) person _______________

c) video _______________ d) lunch _______________

e) key _______________ f) tomato _______________

g) baby _______________ h) wolf _______________

i) deer _______________ j) mouse _______________

k) brush _______________ l) shelf _______________

m) knife _______________ n) goose _______________

5. In each sentence, circle the correct **possessive noun**.

a) Your (sleefs sleeves) are worn out at the elbows.

b) My friends came over to watch some new (videoes videos) with me.

c) The parents watched the (children childrens) perform their play.

d) My voice (echoes echos) when I yell into the cave.

e) That squirrel has run across all the (rooves roofs) on my street.

f) The dentist said my (tooths teeth) are in great shape.

g) I would like some (tomatoes tomatos) in my salad, please.

h) The (ponys ponies) raced each other around the field.

© Chalkboard Publishing

Singular Possessive Nouns

A **possessive noun** shows who or what something belongs to. Add an **apostrophe** (') **+ s** to a **singular noun** to show belonging. Below are two examples of **singular possessive nouns**.

	Singular Possessive Nouns
the coat that belongs to my father	*my **father's** coat*
the mittens that belong to Carla	***Carla's** mittens*

1. Write the **singular possessive noun** for each example below.

   a) the shoes that belong to Amira   __________________ shoes

   b) the nest that belongs to the bird   the __________________ nest

   c) the marbles that belong to Omar   __________________ marbles

   d) the scarf that belongs to the woman   the __________________ scarf

2. Rewrite each sentence. Use a **singular possessive noun** to replace the underlined words in each sentence.

   Example: He painted the legs <u>of the table</u>.
   *He painted the **table's** legs.*

   a) Mario turned the pages <u>of the book</u>.

   ____

   b) The handle <u>of the mug</u> broke off.

   ____

   c) The leaves <u>of the plant</u> turned brown.

   ____

Plural Possessive Nouns

Most **plural nouns** end with *s*. Add an **apostrophe** (') **after the** *s* to make a **plural possessive noun**. Below are some examples.

	Plural Possessive Nouns
the hats that belong to the girls	the **girls'** hats
the barking of the dogs	the **dogs'** barking
the leaves of the trees	the **trees'** leaves

Some **plural nouns** do not end with *s*.
Examples: children   women   men   people

Add an **apostrophe** (') **+ s** to turn these plural nouns into **plural possessive nouns.**
Examples: children's   women's   men's   people's

1. Write the **plural possessive noun** for each example below.

a) the coats that belong to my sisters   my _________________ coats

b) the cat that belongs to my cousins   my _________________ cat

c) the honking of the cars   the _________________ honking

d) the roars of the lions   the _________________ roars

2. Write the **plural possessive noun** for each example below.

a) the laughter of the people   the _________________ laughter

b) the toys belonging to the children   the _________________ toys

c) the gloves belonging to the men   the _________________ gloves

d) the bikes belonging to the women   the _________________ bikes

© Chalkboard Publishing

More Practice with Possessive Nouns

Use a **possessive noun** to show who or what something belongs to. Change a **singular** noun into a **possessive** noun by adding an **apostrophe** (') **+ s**. Look at the examples in the chart below.

Singular Noun	Possessive Noun	Example Sentence
Anne	*Anne's*	***Anne's** new glasses look nice.*
dog	*dog's*	*The **dog's** paws are muddy.*
car	*car's*	*The **car's** horn is very loud!*

1. Rewrite each sentence. Use a **singular possessive noun.** Look at the examples below.

   Examples: The handle <u>of the cup</u> is broken.   *I like the kitten <u>that belongs to Tim</u>.*
   The cup's handle is broken.   *I like Tim's kitten.*

   a) The front tire <u>of my bike</u> is flat.

   ____

   b) Please give me the phone number <u>of the store</u>.

   ____

   c) Did you find the pencil <u>that belongs to Suki</u>?

   ____

   d) This is the watch <u>that belongs to my father</u>.

   ____

   e) The feet <u>of the elephant</u> are huge!

   ____

How do you change a **plural noun** into a **possessive** noun?

If the **plural** noun ends with an *s*, add an **apostrophe** (').

If the **plural** noun does **not** end with an *s*, add an **apostrophe** (') + *s*.

Look at the examples in the chart below.

Plural Noun	Possessive Noun	Example Sentence
sisters	sisters'	My **sisters'** shoes got wet in the rain.
children	children's	The **children's** parents are coming.

2. Rewrite each sentence. Use a **plural possessive noun.** Look at the examples below.

Examples:

I found the hats <u>that belong to the men</u>.   *The windows <u>of the cars</u> are dirty.*
I found the men's hats.   *The cars' windows are dirty.*

a) The leaves <u>of the trees</u> change color in the fall.

____

b) The lids <u>of the jars</u> are in the top drawer.

____

c) The cars <u>that belong to the people</u> are parked outside.

____

d) The coats <u>that belong to my brothers</u> are in the closet.

____

e) We could hear the voices <u>of the women</u>.

____

     © Chalkboard Publishing

Possessive Nouns Review Quiz

1. In each sentence, circle the correct **possessive noun**. Think about whether the sentence needs a **singular** or **plural** possessive noun.

   a) This (shirt's shirts') sleeves are too short for me.

   b) I put away the (puppy's puppies') toys while they were playing outside.

   c) The (children's childrens') teacher taught them a new song.

   d) Dad found (Kim's Kims') mittens on the floor of the hall closet.

   e) Both my (shoe's shoes') laces had come untied.

   f) My baseball (team's teams') uniforms are green and white.

   g) (Kayla's Kaylas') brothers told us some funny jokes.

2. Read each sentence and underline each **possessive noun**. If the possessive noun is **correct**, put a check mark above it. If it is **not correct**, cross it out and write the correct possessive noun above it.

   a) The plant's leaves turned brown when we forgot to water them.

   b) This bird's feathers will get darker when it is older.

   c) My parents met Liams' parents at the school play.

   d) My two sister's eyes are blue, and my eyes are brown.

   e) Jeremy's sweater got caught in his coats' zipper.

   f) The womens' team played first, and the men's team played next.

   g) The markers' caps show what color ink is inside.

Possessive Nouns Review Quiz (continued)

3. Circle the correct **singular possessive noun** in each sentence.

   a) My (aunt's   aunts') fingernails were painted all different colors.

   b) That twisted stick is the (monkeys'   monkey's) favorite toy.

   c) Our (dogs'   dog's) chew bones are buried in the yard.

   d) My (cat's   cats') hairs are all over my pants.

   e) (Jim's   Jims') books are all packed in boxes now.

   f) The (girl's   girls') hair was shiny after she brushed it.

   g) The racing (teams'   team's) helmets matched their clothing.

4. Write the **plural possessive noun** for each example below.

   a) the toys belonging to the children   the _________________ toys

   b) the badges earned by the Scouts   the _________________ badges

   c) the songs of the women   the _________________ songs

   d) the shapes of the clouds   the _________________ shapes

   e) the voices of the people   the _________________ voices

   f) the shirts of the men   the _________________ shirts

   g) the bikes belonging to the racers   the _________________ bikes

© Chalkboard Publishing

Pronouns for People

A **pronoun** is a word that takes the place of one or more nouns.
Use these pronouns to take the place of nouns that name **people**.

I   you   he   she   we   they   him   her   them   us

1. Use a **pronoun** to take the place of the underlined word or words.

   a) <u>Ralph</u> likes horses.

   _____________ likes horses.

   b) <u>The children</u> played hide and seek.

   _____________ played hide and seek.

   c) Emma shared the grapes with <u>Eva and Ravi</u>.

   Emma shared the grapes with _____________.

2. Rewrite each sentence. Change the underlined word or words to a **pronoun**.

   a) <u>Jack and Ana</u> played with the puppies.

   ____

   b) <u>Lu</u> showed the picture to <u>Marc</u>.

   ____

   c) <u>The doctor and the nurse</u> smiled at <u>my sister and me</u>.

   ____

   d) <u>Tanya and I</u> waved goodbye to <u>our aunt and uncle</u>.

   ____

Pronouns for Things

A **pronoun** is a word that takes the place of one or more nouns.

Pronouns take the place of nouns that name **people, places,** or **things.**

Use the pronouns below to take the place of nouns that name **things.**

it they them

1. Use a **pronoun** to take the place of the words in brackets.

   a) Andrew was reading ____________. (the book)

   b) ____________ are bending in the wind. (The trees)

   c) I found ____________ behind the chair. (my mittens)

   d) ____________ have pictures of animals. (The stickers)

2. Rewrite the sentences to use pronouns for **people** and **things.** Change the underlined word or words to a **pronoun.**

   a) <u>The girls</u> gave <u>the toys</u> to <u>San and me</u>.

   ____

   b) <u>The boxes</u> are too big for <u>Alan and Rosa</u> to carry.

   ____

   c) <u>Dave and I</u> sent <u>the birthday card</u> to <u>our grandfather</u>.

   ____

   d) Will <u>Amit and Brittany</u> sing for <u>the visitors</u>?

   ____

© Chalkboard Publishing

Possessive Pronouns

A **pronoun** takes the place of a **noun**. Look at the sentences below.

Example: <u>Angela</u> *waved to* <u>Sami</u>. (*Angela* and *Sami* are nouns).
        <u>She</u> *waved to* <u>him</u>.

She and *him* are **pronouns** that take the place of nouns.

A **possessive pronoun** takes the place of a **possessive noun**.
A **possessive pronoun** shows who or what something belongs to.

Example: Ricardo is <u>Anna's</u> *cousin.* (*Anna's* is a possessive noun.)
        Ricardo is <u>her</u> *cousin.*

Her is a **possessive pronoun** that takes the place of *Anna's.*

Use the **possessive pronouns** below before nouns.

my   your   his   her   its   our   their

---

1. Circle the **possessive pronouns**. Remember that a possessive pronoun shows who or what something belongs to.

a) Eva said, "This loud noise is hurting my ears!"

b) The wind blew the hat off his head.

c) The two birds flew back to their nest in the tree.

d) "Is your mother home from work yet?" asked Mrs. Winters.

e) My brother and I take our shoes off when we go in the house.

f) This sweater is missing two of its buttons.

g) Linda put the notebook in her backpack.

h) Our neighbors are going to sell their house.

2. Rewrite each sentence. Replace the underlined **possessive noun** with a **possessive pronoun**.

a) Frank scratched <u>Frank's</u> nose because it was itchy.

____

b) We are going to have dinner at <u>Aunt Selma's</u> house.

____

c) The Smiths saw birds eating from <u>the Smiths'</u> bird feeder.

____

d) <u>The clock's</u> batteries are dead.

____

e) "Emilio, is it <u>Emilio's</u> birthday today?" Gary asked.

____

f) The teachers said, "It is <u>the teachers'</u> job to help you learn."

____

g) Gail said, "You can borrow <u>Gail's</u> eraser."

____

h) The toy truck is missing one of <u>the truck's</u> wheels.

____

© Chalkboard Publishing

More Possessive Pronouns

Sometimes, **possessive pronouns** do **not** come before a noun. Look at the examples below.

Example: This book is <u>my book</u>.

The possessive pronoun *my* comes before the noun *book*.

Example: This book is <u>mine</u>.

Mine is a **possessive pronoun** that takes the place of *my book*.
Mine **does not** come before a noun.

Example: I drank my milk, but Sasha did not drink <u>her milk</u>.
       I drank my milk, but Sasha did not drink <u>hers</u>.
Hers is a **possessive pronoun** that takes the place of *her milk*.

Hers **does not** come before a noun.

The possessive pronouns below **do not** have to come before a noun.

mine   yours   his   hers   ours   theirs

1. Underline the **possessive pronouns** that come **before** a noun. Circle the **possessive pronouns** that **do not** come before a noun.

   a) I asked Amit if this is his mitten. He said, "It is not mine."

   b) Gail finished writing her story, but Julio is still writing his.

   c) Todd and Leanne both drew pictures of bears. "Yours is just as nice as hers," the teacher told Todd.

   d) Dad liked the color the neighbors painted their house. "We should paint ours the same color as theirs," he said.

   e) Emma and Andrew have toy robots. Hers makes sounds and his has flashing lights.

Did you notice which possessive pronoun in these questions sometimes comes before a noun and sometimes does not? Which one is it?

2. Rewrite each sentence. Replace the underlined words with the correct **possessive pronoun**.

a) My brother's feet are bigger than <u>my feet</u>.

____

b) Our dog barks louder than <u>their dog</u>.

____

c) I think your joke is funnier than <u>John's joke</u>.

____

d) Are these <u>Mom's keys</u> or <u>Dad's keys</u>?

____

3. Circle the correct **possessive pronoun** in the brackets.

a) We think (our ours) team is better than (their theirs).

b) (Your Yours) sweater has stripes, and (my mine) does, too!

c) (My Mine) pen ran out of ink, so may I borrow (your yours)?

d) My uncle grows beautiful roses in his garden, and we grow vegetables in (our ours).

e) My sister's bedroom is bigger than (my mine), but I like (my mine) better than (her hers).

f) Is (your yours) apartment on a higher floor than (their theirs)?

© Chalkboard Publishing

Pronouns Review Quiz

1. Rewrite each sentence. Use a **pronoun** to replace each **underlined word** or **group of words**.

   a) My name is Eddie, and <u>Eddie</u> can help you.

   ____

   b) <u>My friends and I</u> worked hard on our project.

   ____

   c) Please put <u>the ice cubes</u> in the freezer.

   ____

   d) <u>The girls</u> gave <u>Peter</u> a birthday card.

   ____

   e) <u>Sally</u> has already returned <u>the books</u> to <u>Tony and me</u>.

   ____

   f) <u>The shoes</u> are too big for <u>Emma</u>.

   ____

   g) <u>This book</u> is not too hard for <u>the boys</u> to read.

   ____

   h) <u>Marco</u> gave one apple to each of <u>the children</u>.

   ____

2. In each sentence, write the correct **possessive pronoun** to replace the word or words in brackets.

a) ____________ new radio is on the kitchen table. (Uncle Harry's)

b) I see ___________ writing on ___________ pages. (Mom's; the book's)

c) Can we give the cats ____________ food now? (the cats')

d) Ken said, "___________ bicycle has a flat tire!" (Ken's)

e) ___________ feet are sore from walking so far. (My sister's and my)

f) I told Ping, "___________ socks are very colorful!" (Ping's)

g) All _____________ branches are covered with flowers. (the trees')

3. Rewrite each sentence. Replace the **underlined words** with a **possessive pronoun**.

a) <u>Your legs</u> are longer than <u>my legs</u>.

____

b) <u>His frog</u> can jump farther than <u>her frog</u>.

____

c) <u>Our apartment</u> is on a higher floor than <u>their apartment</u>.

____

d) <u>Her bedroom</u> is messier than <u>my bedroom</u>.

____

© Chalkboard Publishing

What Is an Adjective?

An **adjective** is a word that describes a noun.

Example: A big lion ran after me!

The word *big* is an adjective. It describes the noun *lion*.

1. Circle the **adjective** in each sentence. Underline the **noun** it describes.

   a) A brown mouse ran over the carpet.

   b) Mr. Tanaka gave me a large book.

   c) A scary dragon lived in the cave.

   d) The playful puppy ran after me.

   e) Please pass me the green mug.

   f) I fell on the slippery ice.

   g) The loud thunder woke me up.

   h) She watched an interesting movie with Jack.

   i) Carol told me a funny joke.

   j) They put the presents on the round table.

   k) I want to climb a tall mountain.

   l) Bob washed the dirty dishes.

   m) Rachel walked down the lonely road.

   n) The rabbit leaped through the tall grass.

   o) Dave did his happy dance.

   p) The colorful pigeons cooed softly.

   q) The angry cat chased our dog.

2. In each sentence below, write an **adjective** that makes sense. Underline the **noun** your adjective describes.

a) I think I will wear the _____________________ socks today.

b) Pedro spoke in a _____________________ voice.

c) There were _____________________ clouds in the sky.

d) A _____________________ runner will win the race.

e) Dad put the _____________________ flowers in a vase.

f) The _____________________ cat chased a mouse.

g) The _____________________ dog did not move when Mom swept.

3. Circle the **adjective** in brackets that fits best.

a) Wanda put a (round   heavy) book in her backpack.

b) The (yellow   warm) fire melted the snow on her clothes.

c) The (bright   loud) lightning lit up the room.

d) The author had some (great   old) ideas for a new book.

e) Tom left his (worst   favorite) pen at school today.

f) The (sleepy   striped) cat curled up in the (yellow   warm) sunshine.

g) The (pretty   dim) lights sparkled in the (cold   dark) night.

© Chalkboard Publishing

Adjectives Before and After Nouns

An **adjective** describes a noun. Sometimes an adjective comes **before** the noun it describes. Sometimes the adjective comes **after** the noun.

Examples: **Before a noun:** *We walked across the shiny floor.*

After a noun: *The floor was shiny.*

1. Circle the **adjective** in each sentence. Underline the **noun** it describes.

   a) The clown was funny.

   b) Do not cross the street when the light is red.

   c) The woman was angry when the dog chased a cat.

   d) Do you think the towels are dry?

   e) The video Ali watched was exciting.

   f) The pillow I sleep on is soft.

   g) The baby in the crib is cute.

   h) Mr. Rossi makes sandwiches that are delicious.

   i) I wear sunglasses when the sun is bright.

   j) We did not go swimming because the water was cold.

   k) Enzo was tired after he played soccer.

   l) Mrs. Jones told me that the answer is correct.

2. Circle each **adjective** and underline each **noun**. Draw an arrow from each adjective to the noun it describes.

   Example: The old man wore a scarf that was yellow.

   a) The huge dinosaur had teeth that were sharp.

   b) The children were happy when the colorful rainbow appeared.

   c) A woman who was tall fixed our leaky roof.

Adjectives Can Describe How Many

An **adjective** describes a noun. Some adjectives answer the question "How many?"
Numbers can be adjectives.

Example: I popped three balloons!

In this sentence, *three* is an **adjective** that describes the noun **balloons**.
The adjective *three* answers the question "How many balloons?"

Some **adjectives** answer the question "How many?" but they do not tell exactly how many.

Example: I have some questions for you.

In this sentence, *some* is an **adjective** that describes the noun *questions. Some* does not tell exactly how many questions, but it tells us there are more than one.

1. Circle the **adjectives** and underline **all** the **nouns**. Draw an arrow from each adjective to the **noun it describes**.

   a) Three apples fell from the tree.

   b) Raj found four coins under the bed.

   c) Sandra watched two squirrels climb a tree.

   d) Eight frogs hopped into the pond.

2. Circle each **adjective** that answers the question "How many?"

   a) I returned several books to the library.

   b) Many students are absent today.

   c) Few people keep snakes as pets.

   d) We watched some airplanes land at the airport.

   e) There were many cows on the farm, but I saw few horses.

   f) I have collected several seashells and many rocks.

© Chalkboard Publishing

Using Adjectives to Compare Two Things

You can use an **adjective** to **compare two things**.

Example: Sam is <u>taller</u> than Ali.

This sentence compares how tall Sam and Ali are.

For many adjectives that have **one syllable**, just add *er* to make an adjective that compares two things.

Examples: fast – faster   short – shorter

For these adjectives, double the **final consonant** before adding *er*.
hot – hotter   big – bigger   fat – fatter   sad – sadder

1. Complete each sentence. Change the **adjective** in brackets to make it **compare two things**.

   a) My brother is _____________________ than my sister. (old)

   b) The green book is _________________ than the red book. (thick)

   c) A dime is _______________ than a quarter. (small)

   d) January is _______________ than June. (cold)

   e) The sun is _________________ than the moon. (bright)

   f) The kitchen is _________________ than the basement. (warm)

   g) My new pillow is _______________ than my old pillow. (soft)

2. Complete each sentence. Change the **adjective** in brackets to make it **compare two things**.

   a) Henry was _______________ than Tina when it was time to go. (sad)

   b) Today is _______________ than yesterday. (hot)

   c) My cat is _______________ than your cat. (fat)

   d) A truck is _______________ than a car. (big)

Using Adjectives to Compare More Than Two Things

You can use adjectives to compare **more than two things**.

Example: Anna is the tallest student in the class.

This sentence **compares** all the students in the class. Anna is the tallest.

For most adjectives that have one syllable, add **est** to make an adjective that compares **more than two things**.

Example: short – shortest

1. Use the **adjective** in brackets to complete the first sentence in each pair. Use the correct form of the adjective to compare **more than two things**. Then complete the second sentence to tell what is being compared.

   a) Lily was the _________________ runner in the race. (fast)

   This sentence compares all the ____.

   b) Today is the _________________ day of the year. (cold)

   This sentence compares all the ____.

   c) This is the _________________ coat in my closet. (warm)

   This sentence compares _________________________________ in my closet.

   d) My bed is the _________________ bed in the house. (soft)

   This sentence compares _________________________________ in the house.

2. Use the **adjective** in brackets to compare **more than two things**. Remember to write **the** before an adjective that ends with **est.**

   a) The red truck is _________________________ truck in the garage. (clean)

   b) This lightbulb is _________________________ lightbulb we have. (bright)

   c) The dictionary is _________________________ book on the shelf. (thick)

   d) I took _________________________ muffin on the plate. (small)

 © Chalkboard Publishing

Tricky Adjectives That Compare

Watch out for these tricky adjectives that compare!

Adjective	To Compare Two Things	To Compare More Than Two Things
good	*better*	*best*
bad	*worse*	*worst*
far	*farther*	*farthest*
many	*more*	*most*

Use the **adjective** in brackets to complete the first sentence in the pair. Then circle the correct answer in the second sentence. Write **the** before an adjective that compares **more than two things.**

a) The story about dragons was _________________ than the story about dinosaurs. (good)

   This sentence compares (two things   more than two things).

b) Do you think a sore throat is _________________ than a cough? (bad)

   This sentence compares (two things   more than two things).

c) Hockey and baseball are good, but I think soccer is _________________ sport. (good)

   This sentence compares (two things   more than two things).

d) Your house is _________________ from school than my house. (far)

   This sentence compares (two things   more than two things).

e) Of all the classes in our school, Mr. Rico's class has _________________ students. (many)

   This sentence compares (two things   more than two things).

f) There were some bad storms last year, but this storm is _________________. (bad)

   This sentence compares (two things   more than two things).

Adjectives That Use *More* and *Most* to Compare

For most adjectives that have **two or more syllables**, use *more* to compare **two things**. Use *the most* to compare **more than two things**.

Compare Two Things	Compare More Than Two Things
Karen is <u>more</u> helpful than Bill.	*Johnny is <u>the most</u> helpful of all the children in the class.*

Watch out for adjectives that have **two** syllables, and **end with y**. For these adjectives, change the **y** to **i** and add **er** or **est** when you want to compare.

Examples: *shiny – shinier – shiniest   easy – easier – easiest*
hungry – hungrier – hungriest   healthy – healthier – healthiest

1. Read each sentence and think about how many things are compared. Complete the sentence by writing *more* or *the most.*

   a) Liz was frightened, but Larry was _________________ frightened.

   b) We saw elephants and giraffes, but I thought the monkeys were _______________ interesting animals at the zoo.

   c) Bob thinks apples are _______________ delicious than bananas.

   d) Of all the women at the ball, Prince Charming thought Cinderella was

   _____________________ beautiful.

2. Use the correct form of the word in brackets to compare. Remember to use *the* with words ending in *est*.

   a) The old tabby cat is _________________ cat in the neighborhood. (grumpy)

   b) Cindy's dog is _________________ than my dog. (hairy)

   c) Today, my brother is acting _____________________ he's ever acted. (silly)

   d) That sheep has _____________________ coat I've ever seen. (curly)

     © Chalkboard Publishing

Make an Adjective Poem

Cut out and paste a picture of a person, place, or thing from a magazine onto the middle of the space below. Write adjectives around the picture to describe what you have chosen and to create a poem. The first word in the poem should name the person, place, or thing you have chosen.

Using the Articles *A*, *An*, and *The*

The words **a**, **an**, and ***the*** are called **articles**. Use **a** before a **singular noun** that starts with a **consonant**. Use **an** before a **singular noun** that starts with a **vowel**. Look at the examples below.

Examples: **a** *monkey*   **a** *river*   **a** *washer*
          an *eel*   **an** *arrow*   **an** *octopus*

Use ***the*** before a **singular** or **plural noun**.

Examples: ***the*** *pipe*   ***the*** *dress*   ***the*** *snakes*   ***the*** *elephants*

Choosing Between *A*, *An*, and *The*

Use ***the*** when you are talking about something **specific**. A specific thing is **one particular example**.

Example: <u>**The** car</u> *parked on the road does not belong to us.*

This sentence is not about just any car. It is about one particular example of a car—the car that is parked on the road. The writer used ***the*** to talk about a **specific** car.

A **specific** example can include **more than one** thing.

Example: <u>**The** sailboats</u> *we saw at the marina were beautiful.*

This sentence is not about just any sailboats. It is about the particular sailboats the writer saw at the marina. The writer used ***the*** to talk about a **specific** example of a group of sailboats.

Use **a** or **an** when you are talking about something **in general**. That means you are **not** talking about a **specific** example.

Example: We went to the animal shelter to adopt <u>***a*** *puppy*</u>*.*

The writer is talking about a puppy **in general**. There is **not** one specific example of a puppy that the writer has already seen and has decided to get.

Example: We went to the animal shelter to adopt <u>***the*** *puppy*</u> *we saw there yesterday.*

This sentence is about a **specific** example of a puppy, so the writer used ***the*** instead of **a**.

© Chalkboard Publishing

Using the Articles *A*, *An*, and *The* (continued)

Sometimes, a **singular noun** has an **adjective** in front of it. If the sentence is **not** talking about a **specific** example and the adjective starts with a **vowel**, use *an*.

Examples: **an** *old book*   **an** *easy puzzle*   **an** *interesting idea*

If the **singular noun** is **not** a specific example and the **adjective** starts with a **consonant**, use *a* even if the noun starts with a vowel.

Examples: **a** *happy child*   **a** *blue ball*   **a** *frisky dog*

Write the correct word (*a, an,* or *the*) in each sentence. Think about whether the sentence is about something **specific** or something **general**.

a) We are all excited about visiting my cousins at ______ cottage.

b) There is _____ eagle on the American quarter.

c) When we go to the zoo, I always want to see _____ elephants.

d) I read that ____ emu is taller than my father.

e) _____ baby's blanket was all wet.

f) Jeff rides _____ bicycle in _____ park.

g) My sister wants _____ apple and I want _____ pear.

h) I can spin _____ nickel, but I cannot spin _____ dime.

i) Cara drew _____ picture of _____ apple tree.

j) Tim went to _____ park to play on _____ swings.

k) ____ squirrel that lives in our tree made _____ pile of acorns under ____ oak tree.

l) I went to _____ library to return ____ book I borrowed last week.

m) _____ bear walked into _____ woods and ate _____ amazing amount of berries.

Adjectives and Articles Review Quiz

1. Circle each **adjective** and underline each **noun**. Draw an arrow from each **adjective** to the **noun** it describes.

   a) The old man lived in a big house beside a beautiful lake.

   b) The wet floor was slippery.

   c) The soup is hot and delicious.

   d) Two women sat in chairs under a tall tree.

   e) Many children like funny stories better than scary stories.

   f) Several people brought some snacks to the party.

   g) Few guests came late, and four people came early.

   h) The little boy with red hair is tired.

2. In each sentence, circle the correct way to use **adjectives** to compare.

   a) Taylor swims fast, but Jenny swims (faster the fastest).

   b) The children in the choir sang loud, but Tim sang (louder the loudest).

   c) These two snakes are long, but the green one is (longer the longest).

   d) Mom and I both have short hair, but my hair is (shorter the shortest).

   e) Of all the children on my team, Kyle is (taller the tallest).

   f) Tom and Leah are hungry, but I am (hungrier the hungriest).

   g) My two sisters are funny, but my older sister is (funnier the funniest).

© Chalkboard Publishing

3. In each sentence, circle the correct way to **compare** two or more things.

   a) Roberto was frightened, but his sister was (more the most) frightened.

   b) I tasted three soups, and the chicken soup was (more the most) delicious.

   c) The book has seven chapters, and the last chapter is (more the most) interesting.

   d) My dad's garden and my grandmother's garden are both beautiful, but my grandmother's garden is (more the most) beautiful.

   e) I have seen many movies, but this movie is (more the most) exciting one I have ever seen.

   f) The second question on the quiz is (more the most) difficult than the first question.

4. Complete the sentences with the correct word—**a**, **an**, or **the**.

   a) The Millers hope to buy _______ house somewhere near a lake.

   b) Let us see if the library has _______ book this movie is based on.

   c) I want to find a place where I can buy _______ sandwich for lunch.

   d) Do you have _______ extra pencil I can borrow?

   e) He needs to buy _______ lightbulb to put in this lamp.

   f) I have one sock, but I do not know where _______ matching one is.

   g) When we go to Africa, we hope to see _______ elephant.

What Is a Verb?

A **verb** is a word that tells what someone or something is doing.
In the sentences below, the verbs are underlined.

Examples: Karen <u>reaches</u> for the book.   The glass <u>falls</u> to the floor.

1. Circle the **verb** in each sentence.

   a) Justin jumps over the puddle.

   b) The bird flies far away.

   c) Eliza gives an apple to her sister.

   d) Lightning flashes across the sky.

   e) He forgets my name all the time.

   f) My grandmother sends me a birthday card every year.

   g) I see a nest in that tree!

   h) That door squeaks when you open it.

   i) Carla and Frank dance to the music.

   j) The happy sheep runs down the hill.

2. Circle the all the **verbs** in each group of words.

   a) wood   rug   tells   spiders   cleans

   b) writes   pencil   erasers   penny   says

   c) builds   roads   explores   garbage   tea

   d) windows   sports   hears   hides   bush

   e) buys   medicine   rainbows   scarf   pours

   f) remembers   pillows   asks   scrubs   suitcase

   g) skips   sidewalk   decides   kittens   shoes

   © Chalkboard Publishing

Make a Verb Collage

Cut out pictures from magazines and fliers that represent verbs, and paste them below.

The Verbs *Be*, *Do*, and *Have*

Below are the **present tense** forms of the verbs *be*, *do*, and *have*.

Be	Do	Have
I am	*I do*	*I have*
he is, she is, it is	*he does, she does, it does*	*he has, she has, it has*
we are, you are, they are	*we do, you do, they do*	*we have, you have, they have*

1. Write the correct **present tense** form of the verb *be*.

    a) It _______ amazing that you got here so quickly.

    b) They _______ sad that they will not be able to come with us.

    c) I _______ sure I will score a goal in the game tonight.

    d) You _______ very lucky to have such a good friend.

2. Write the correct **present tense** form of the verb *do*.

    a) We _________ not drop litter on the ground.

    b) He always _________ his homework after supper.

    c) Sometimes, I _________ exercises to help me stay fit.

    d) It _________ a good job of vacuuming up dirt and dust.

3. Write the correct **present tense** form of the verb *have*.

    a) They __________ seven fish in their aquarium.

    b) I __________ long red hair and blue eyes.

    c) She __________ a pencil case just like mine.

    d) You __________ some very interesting ideas!

© Chalkboard Publishing

The Verbs *Be*, *Do*, and *Have* (continued)

Below are the **past tense** forms of the verbs *be*, *do*, and *have*.

Be	Do	Have
I was, he *was*, she *was*, it was	*I did, he did, she did, it did*	*I had, he had, she had, it had*
we *were*, you *were*, they *were*	we *did*, you *did*, they *did*	we *had*, you *had*, they *had*

4. Circle the correct **past tense** form of the verb in brackets.

a) He (was   were) very excited about going to the zoo.

b) She (has   had) a cold last week, but she feels better now.

c) We (do   did) all of the chores on our list.

d) It (had   has) three buttons, but one button fell off.

e) You (was   were) right, and I (was   were) wrong.

f) They (has   had) three cats, but they gave one to us.

5. Choose the correct verb (*be*, *do*, or *have*). Then write the correct **past tense** form of the verb.

a) It _____________ a sunny day when we went hiking last week.

b) They _____________ all the work in a very short time.

c) He _____________ several coins in the pocket of his jeans.

d) They _____________ on the top shelf the last time I looked.

e) We _____________ lots of fun playing tag with the other children.

f) You _____________ very helpful to me when I had a broken arm.

More Practice with *Be*, *Do*, and *Have*

Review the **present tense** and **past tense** forms of the verbs *be*, *do*, and *have*.

Present Tense

	Be	Do	Have
I	*am*	*do*	*have*
he, she, it	*is*	*does*	*has*
we, you, they	*are*	*do*	*have*

Past Tense

	Be	Do	Have
I, he, she, it	*was*	*did*	*had*
we, you, they	*were*	*did*	*had*

1. Look at the **verb** in bold. Is it in the **present tense** or **past tense**? Circle your answer, then **check** the charts above to see if your answer is correct.

   a) We **were** all excited about going to the circus.   **present past**

   b) I wonder if she **is** still at home.   **present past**

   c) They **had** lots of fun at the amusement park.   **present past**

   d) He **did** the grocery shopping this morning.   **present past**

   e) It **has** a power button to turn the television on or off.   **present past**

   f) You **are** always on time for basketball practice.   **present past**

   g) She **was** interested in learning more about whales.   **present past**

   h) We **do** the dishes as soon as we have finished eating.   **present past**

   i) My best friend **does** lots of favors for me.   **present past**

© Chalkboard Publishing

2. Read each sentence and decide whether it needs a **present tense** or **past tense** verb. Then write the **correct form** of the verb in brackets.

a) Last year, she ___________ in Grade 2. (be)

b) Now you ___________ five minutes left to finish the quiz. (have)

c) He ___________ the laundry last Wednesday. (do)

d) We ___________ very busy all day yesterday. (be)

e) I ___________ happy because my grandparents are visiting. (be)

f) You still ___________ lots of time to do your homework now. (have)

g) They ___________ two word search puzzles last night. (do)

3. Read each sentence and decide whether it needs a **present tense verb** or a **past tense verb**. Then choose the correct verb (**be**, **do**, or **have**) and write the **correct form** of the verb.

a) Last month, it ___________ cloudy almost every day.

b) She ________ some stretches to warm up before the race started.

c) I ___________ a cut on my finger, but it will heal soon.

d) It is almost lunchtime, so we ___________ hungry.

e) They ___________ no trouble falling asleep last night.

f) He ___________ a jigsaw puzzle, then he cleaned his room.

g) You ___________ a better goalie now than you were last year.

h) We ________ our homework before we watched the movie.

i) He used to have one cat, but now he ___________ two.

Linking Verbs

A **linking verb** is a verb that does **not** show **action**.
The verb *be* is a linking verb.

Remember that the verb *be* has different forms.
The **present tense** forms of *be* are *am*, *is*, and *are*.
The **past tense** forms of *be* are *was* and *were*.

Compare the **verbs** in the example sentences below.

*Example: Shauna **kicks** the ball.*
Kicks is an action, so ***kicks*** is an action verb.

*Example: The twins **are** eight years old.*
Are is **not** an action, so ***are*** is **not** an action verb. ***Are*** is a **linking verb**. (Remember that ***are*** is a present tense form of the verb ***be**.)

A **linking verb** connects the **subject** of the sentence (the person or thing the sentence is about) to a **noun** or an **adjective**. Look at the examples below.

*Example: This <u>girl</u> **is** my <u>cousin</u>.*
The linking verb *is* connects the **subject** of the sentence (*girl*) to a **noun** (*cousin*).

*Example: The <u>children</u> **were** <u>hungry</u>.*
The linking verb ***were*** connects the **subject** of the sentence (*children*) to an **adjective** (*hungry*).

*Example: <u>Mr. Wilson</u> **was** a <u>teacher</u>.*
The linking verb ***was*** connects the **subject** of the sentence (*Mr. Wilson*) to a **noun** (*teacher*).

*Example: <u>We</u> **are** <u>excited</u>.*
The linking verb ***are*** connects the **subject** of the sentence (*We*) to an **adjective** (*excited*).

© Chalkboard Publishing

Linking Verbs (continued)

1. In the sentences below, the **verbs** are in bold. Circle all the **linking** verbs. Underline all the **action** verbs.

   a) The windows **were** dirty.

   b) Lisa **ran** all the way home.

   c) This joke **is** funny.

   d) These flowers **are** colorful.

   e) The glass **fell** off the table.

   f) I **am** tired today.

2. Find the **verbs** in the sentences below. Circle all the **linking** verbs. Underline all the **action** verbs.

   a) Mr. Yang painted a beautiful picture. He is an artist.

   b) These grapes are delicious. Let us eat some more.

   c) All the flowers were lovely. I picked a red flower for Mom.

   d) I am a carpenter. I build cupboards and shelves.

   e) My little puppy is cute. It was a gift from my parents.

   f) Angela slipped on some ice. She fell on the sidewalk.

   g) The movies were funny. We laughed a lot!

   h) These pictures are nice. The children drew them.

   i) We swam in the lake. The water was very cold!

   j) I am excited. Today is my birthday!

Spelling Present Tense Verbs

For most **present tense** verbs, add **s** if **he**, **she**, or **it** does the action.

Watch out for verbs that need tricky spelling changes!

For verbs that end in a **consonant + y**, change the **y** to **i** and add **es**.

Examples: I study – she studies   they carry – he carries

For verbs that end with **s**, **x**, **ch**, or **sh**, add **es**.

Examples: I kiss – she kisses   I fix – he fixes
*   they pinch – it pinches   you wish – he wishes*

1. In the blank, write the correct **present tense** of the verb in brackets.

   a) She _______________ the words from the board. (copy)

   b) The little boy _____________ because he is scared. (cry)

   c) Max _______________ carrots and onions. (buy)

   d) The kite _______________ in the wind. (fly)

   e) The raccoon ________________ to climb over the fence. (try)

2. In the blank, write the correct **present tense** of the verb in brackets.

   a) My brother ________________ his mosquito bite. (scratch)

   b) Alice ________________ the button on the elevator. (push)

   c) Marcus __________________ the stack of papers. (pass)

   d) She ___________________ the flour and fruit together. (mix)

   e) The bucket _________________ the drops of water. (catch)

   © Chalkboard Publishing

Past Tense Verbs

Past tense verbs tell what happened in the **past.** Look at these examples:

Verb	Present Tense	Past Tense
talk	Today, I talk.	Yesterday, I talked.
	Today, she talks.	Yesterday, she talked.

For many verbs, add **ed** to the verb to make the past tense.
If the verb already ends with **e**, just add **d**.

1. Write the **past tense** of the verbs below. Add **ed** or **d** to make the past tense.

    a) invent _________________________   b) cough _________________________

    c) share _________________________   d) work _________________________

    e) borrow _________________________   f) escape _________________________

    g) agree _________________________   h) explode _________________________

2. Complete each sentence. Write the **past tense** of the verb in brackets to show that the action happened in the past.

    a) The dog _________________________ the squirrel. (chase)

    b) Leon _________________________ his food slowly. (chew)

    c) Kelly _________________________ the sink with water. (fill)

3. Is the verb in each sentence **present tense** or **past tense**? Write **present** or **past** beside each sentence.

    a) Mom glued the pieces back together. _________________________

    b) We race along the path through the park. _________________________

    c) Jonathan rinses the shampoo out of his hair. _________________________

Spelling Past Tense Verbs

For many verbs that end with **consonant + vowel + consonant**, double the final consonant before adding *ed*.

Examples: *hop – hopped*　　　*clap – clapped*　　　*zip – zipped*

For most verbs that end with a **consonant + y**, change the *y* to an *i* and add *ed*.

Examples: *study – studied*　　　*marry – married*

1. Write the **past tense** of the verb in brackets. For each verb, double the final consonant before adding *ed*.

a) Jeremy _________________ on a rock. (trip)

b) The car _________________ at the red light. (stop)

c) Dad made the soup, and I _________________ it. (stir)

d) Ella _________________ paint on the floor. (drip)

e) Richard _________________ over the puddle. (step)

2. Write the **past tense** of the verb in brackets.

a) The baby _________________ when he dropped his rattle. (cry)

b) The movers _________________ the heavy boxes. (carry)

c) They _________________ to the party. (hurry)

d) Eva _________________ about her lost dog. (worry)

© Chalkboard Publishing

Tricky Past Tense Verbs

The **past tense** of some verbs does not end with **ed**. Watch out for these tricky verbs when you use the past tense!

Present Tense	Past Tense
come, comes	came
drive, drives	drove
eat, eats	ate
fall, falls	fell

Present Tense	Past Tense
get, gets	got
give, gives	gave
have, has	had
say, says	said

1. Write the **past tense** of the verb in brackets.

a) Lina _______________ a cold last week. (have)

b) Yesterday, Jacob _______________ he wanted to visit us. (say)

c) Who _______________ all the snacks? (eat)

d) The principal _______________ to our classroom. (come)

2. Rewrite each sentence. Change the **past tense verb** to **present tense**.

a) We drove to the grocery store.

____

b) The squirrel ate all the nuts.

____

c) I had two pencils in my desk.

____

d) Carly came to my house every week.

____

Tricky Past Tense Verbs (continued)

Watch out for these tricky verbs when you use the **past tense**!

Present Tense	Past Tense
buy, buys	brought
draw, draws	drove
drink, drinks	drank
find, finds	found

Present Tense	Past Tense
know, knows	knew
go, goes	went
take, takes	took
think, thinks	thought

3. Write the **past tense** of the verb in brackets.

a) We _______________ along the path through the forest. (go)

b) Brendan _______________ a glass of milk with his sandwich. (drink)

c) I _______________ my answer was correct. (think)

d) Emily _______________ some pretty flowers at the market. (buy)

4. Rewrite each sentence. Change the **past tense verb** to **present tense**.

a) We drank juice with our breakfast.

____

b) He bought a new toy for his grandson.

____

c) Anna found lots of seashells at the beach.

____

d) I thought about my best friend.

____

© Chalkboard Publishing

Future Tense Verbs

Future tense verbs tell about things that will happen in the **future**.
To make future tense verbs, use the helping verb **will**.

One Person or Thing	More Than One Person or Thing
I will walk	We will walk
You will walk	You will walk
He/She/It will walk	They will walk

1. Complete each sentence. Write the **future tense** of the verb in brackets to show that the action will happen in the future.

a) Tomorrow, they _________________________ a horse. (ride)

b) Next week, Sandy _________________________ in the pool. (swim)

c) This morning, the sun _________________________. (shine)

d) In ten minutes, Dad _________________________ me home. (drive)

2. Rewrite each sentence. Change the **past tense** verb to a **future tense** verb.

a) Timothy planted a tree in the backyard.

____

b) Carlos and Mary talked about the movie.

____

c) People laughed at all my silly jokes.

____

Helping Verbs: Present and Future Tenses

A **main verb** tells what someone or something is or does. Look at the example below.

Example: Mr. Silver <u>cooks</u> dinner.

A **helping verb** works with a **main verb** to show action. Use the helping verbs *is*, *am*, and *are* to tell about things that are happening **now**.

In the sentences below, the **main verb** is underlined, and the **helping verb** is in bold. All the sentences tell about an action that is happening **now**.

*Examples: Mr. Jenkins **is** <u>cooking</u> dinner.*
*I **am** <u>cooking</u> dinner.*
*My parents **are** <u>cooking</u> dinner.*

Use the helping verbs *is*, *am*, and *are* with **main verbs** that end with *ing*.

1. Circle the correct **helping verb** in brackets to tell about an action that is happening now. Underline the **main verb** in each sentence.

   a) Paula (is am are) looking for her sunglasses.

   b) The wind (is am are) blowing leaves off the trees.

   c) I (is am are) brushing my teeth.

   d) The dogs (is am are) chasing the cat.

   e) My father (is am are) cutting the grass with the new lawnmower.

   f) Now I (is am are) working on my science project.

   g) We (is am are) pulling weeds from the garden.

   h) My neighbors (is am are) washing their windows.

© Chalkboard Publishing

Use the **helping verb *will*** to tell about things that will happen in the **future**. Look at the examples below.

*Examples: Tony **will** <u>clean</u> his room in a few minutes.*
*Samantha **will** <u>arrive</u> tomorrow afternoon.*

Notice that when you use ***will*** before a **main verb**, the main verb does **not** end with ***ing***.

2. Rewrite each sentence to make the action happen in the **future**. Use the helping verb ***will***. Look at the example below.

Examples: The garbage truck is coming.
The garbage truck will come.

a) The children are planting tulips.

____

b) We hang the pictures on the wall.

____

c) I am singing my favorite song.

____

d) The birds are building a nest in the tree.

____

e) They ask the librarian some questions.

____

Helping Verbs: Past Tense

A **helping verb** works with a **main verb** to show an action. Use the helping verbs **has**, **had**, and **have** to tell about things that have **already happened**. Look at the examples below. The **main verb** is underlined, and the **helping verb** is in bold.

*Examples: The rain **has** <u>stopped</u>.*
*My neighbor **had** <u>painted</u> her house.*
*The students **have** <u>made</u> signs for the bake sale.*

1. Circle the correct **helping verb** in brackets to tell about an action that has already happened. Underline the **main verb** in each sentence.

a) My grandmother (has have) walked to the grocery store.

b) My dog (have had) chewed a hole in my sock.

c) These plants (have has) grown taller since last week.

d) Three apples (has have) dropped from the apple tree.

e) The paint on the picnic table (have has) dried quickly.

f) The car (had have) stopped at the red light.

g) The children (have has) wrapped all the gifts.

h) I (has have) played with the cat earlier that morning.

i) They (have has) built a doghouse for their dog.

j) Julie (have has) invited me to the party.

k) All the snow (had have) melted during the warm weather.

© Chalkboard Publishing

Helping Verbs: Past Tense (continued)

Use the **helping verbs** *was* and *were* to tell about things that have **already happened**. Look at the examples below. The **main verb** is underlined, and the **helping verb** is in bold.

*Examples: My brother **was** <u>helping</u> Mom clean up.*
*The flags **were** <u>flapping</u> in the wind.*

Notice that **was** and **were** are used with **main verbs** that end with **ing**.

2. Circle the correct **helping verb** in brackets to tell about an action that has already happened.

a) The telephone (was were) ringing when I got home.

b) The firefighters (was were) putting out a fire.

c) Some women (was were) watching their children in the park.

d) He (was were) looking at the lightning in the sky.

e) Aunt Joan (was were) raking leaves from her lawn.

f) My new shoes (was were) hurting my feet.

3. Circle the correct **main verb** to use with the **helping verb** in each sentence.

a) Shauna has (walks walked walking) to the library and back.

b) Last night, the crickets were (chirp chirping chirped).

c) He was (climbs climbing climbed) up the oak tree.

d) The cooks were (stir stirring stirred) large pots of soup.

e) I was (collect collecting collected) coins from many different countries.

Subject–Verb Agreement

The **subject** of a **verb** is the person, people, thing, or things doing the action.
In the examples below, the **subject** of the verb is in bold, and the **verb** is underlined.

*Examples: The **children** <u>laugh</u> at the joke.*
*The **child** <u>laughs</u> at the joke*

Notice that in the second sentence above, an *s* is added to the verb *laugh*. Sometimes, you need to change the spelling of a **present tense verb** to make the correct form to use with the **subject**. Here are two more examples:

*Examples: The **men** <u>wash</u> the dog.*
*The **man** <u>washes</u> the dog.*

Notice that sometimes you need to add *es* to a **present tense verb** to make the correct form of the verb for the **subject**.

When the verb is in the **correct form** for the **subject**, we say that the subject and verb "**agree**."

1. Write the correct form of the **verb** in brackets. Make sure the subject and the verb **agree**.

a) The horse _________________ across the field. (run)

b) The moon _________________ at night. (glows)

c) The boats _________________ across the lake. (sails)

d) These weeds _________________ quickly! (grow)

e) Janelle _________________ a mosquito bite. (scratch)

f) The women _________________ for cooler weather. (run)

g) The cat _________________ the mouse across the lawn. (follow)

h) The twins _________________ out their candles. (blows)

© Chalkboard Publishing

2. Circle the correct **present tense** form of the verb to make the subject and verb **agree**.

a) My sister always (study studies) very hard.

b) Snow (fall falls) all day long.

c) The workers (unload unloads) lots of boxes from the truck.

d) Janice (brush brushes) her teeth after every meal.

e) The squirrels (bury buries) acorns in our lawn.

f) The police officers (look looks) for the thieves.

3. Write the correct **present tense** form of the verb in brackets to make the subject and verb **agree**.

a) The doctor _______________ to the sick patient. (rush)

b) Carlos _______________ that show every week. (watch)

c) People _______________ silly things sometimes. (say)

d) The boy _______________ across the puddle. (jump)

e) The children _______________ the national anthem. (sing)

f) Slowly, the caterpillar _______________ across the floor. (creep)

g) After dinner, my brother often _______________ for a walk. (go)

h) My friends sometimes _______________ their bikes in the park. (ride)

i) The angry cat _______________ at the raccoon. (hiss)

Pronoun–Verb Agreement

The **subject** of a **verb** is the person, people, thing, or things doing the action. In the examples below, the **subject** of the verb is in bold, and the **verb** is underlined.

Examples: **Crickets** <u>chirp</u> in the long grass.
The **worker** <u>climbs</u> up the tall ladder.

Sometimes, the **subject** of a verb is a **pronoun**. In the examples below, the **pronoun** that is the **subject** of the verb is in bold, and the **verb** is underlined.

Examples: **He** <u>takes</u> the money off the table.
They <u>give</u> the children some oranges.

When the verb is in the **correct form** for the **subject**, we say that the subject and verb "**agree**."

The **subject** and **verb** always need to **agree**, even when the subject is a **pronoun**. Remember:
• For most **present tense action verbs**, add *s* or *es* if the subject is **he**, **she**, or **it**.
• **Do not** add *s* or *es* if the subject is **I, you, we,** or **they**.

---

1. Write the correct form of the **verb** in brackets. Make sure the subject and the verb **agree**.

   a) It _________________________ the color of your eyes. (match)

   b) We _________________________ lightning in the cloudy sky. (see)

   c) She _________________________ the hole in the roof. (fix)

   d) Suddenly, they _________________________ all the way home. (runs)

   e) I _________________________ all the marbles in the bag. (count)

   f) He _________________________ the dog's toy under the couch. (find)

   g) You _________________________ Jessie your color pencils. (lend)

© Chalkboard Publishing

2. Write the correct **present tense** form of the **verb** in brackets to make the **subject** and **verb agree**.

a) He _________________ the baby on the cheek. (kiss)

b) Sometimes, you _________________ your shoelaces too tightly. (tie)

c) Usually, it _________________ a loud noise when it falls over. (make)

d) She _________________ a muffin for herself and one for her brother. (take)

e) He _________________ the bump on his forehead. (touch)

f) We _________________ a new person has joined our team. (notice)

g) I carefully _________________ each bite of food. (chew)

h) She _________________ the goal on her last shot at the net. (miss)

3. Circle the correct **present tense** form of the verb in brackets to make the **pronoun subject** and the **verb agree**. Then see if you can answer the riddle.

a) It (keep keeps) you warm in bed on chilly nights. What is it? _________________

b) They (make makes) a flashlight's bulb light up. What are they? _________________

c) It (buzz buzzes) to wake you up in the morning. What is it? _________________

d) They (help helps) some people see better. What are they? _________________

e) It (go goes) around your waist. What is it? _________________

f) They (come comes) to put out a fire. What are they? _________________

Verbs Review Quiz 1

1. Circle all the **verbs** in each sentence.

    a) My fingernails grow longer and longer until I cut them.

    b) Our team cheers whenever one of our players hits a home run.

    c) We climb the tree and pick some apples.

    d) I erased the incorrect answer and wrote the correct one.

2. Circle all the **verbs** in each list.

    a) make   stapler   tell   takes   sheet   beautiful

    b) playful   happy   find   sad   ask   job   sees

    c) hard   write   worst   listen   toaster   bring

3. Write the correct **present tense** form of the verb in brackets. (The present tense tells about actions that are happening **now**.)

    a) Dad _____________ the cooking in my family. (do)

    b) She _____________ the leaky tap. (fix)

    c) You _____________ the ball and throw it to Noah. (catch)

    d) It _____________ up in the sky and out into space. (fly)

    e) Sheila ___________ new winter boots at the store. (buy)

    f) The shot _____________ the goal. (miss)

    g) I _____________ the captain of my hockey team. (be)

© Chalkboard Publishing

4. Write the correct **past tense** form of the verb in brackets. (The past tense tells about actions that have **already happened**.)

   a) The man ______________ all the way home in the winter storm. (walk)

   b) The audience ______________ loudly when the play was over. (clap)

   c) Nick ______________ sick all last week. (be)

   d) Some workers ______________ long boards into the new house. (carry)

   e) We ______________ a jigsaw puzzle before we went to bed. (finish)

   f) The truck ______________ slowly down the road. (drive)

   g) They ______________ milk, cheese, and vegetables. (buy)

   h) Nobody ______________ the answer to my question. (know)

   i) The children ______________ excited about going to the circus. (be)

5. Write the correct **future tense** form of the verb in brackets. (The future tense tells about actions that will happen **in the future**.) Remember to use a **helping verb**.

   a) Tomorrow, I ______________ you to tell you what time to come. (call)

   b) Maria ______________ us her story next. (read)

   c) My grandparents ______________ us next week. (visit)

   d) You ______________ even taller next year. (grow)

   e) We ______________ a cake for his birthday. (make)

Verbs Review Quiz 2

1. Circle the **linking** verbs and underline the **action** verbs.

   a) The weather was cold. I found my warm jacket.

   b) I read comic books. They are exciting!

   c) You were sad, so I told you a funny joke.

   d) The television show was good, but the commercials were boring.

2. Circle each **helping verb** and underline each **main verb**.

   a) The rain is making us wet!

   b) The cars were honking at us.

   c) I am running faster than the other people in the race.

   d) You are singing a very pretty song.

3. Write the correct form of the **verb** in brackets. Make sure the subject and the verb **agree**.

   a) The squirrels _______________ up the elm tree. (climbs)

   b) An elephant _______________ its long trunk in different ways. (uses)

   c) He _______________ green eyes and black hair. (have)

   d) You _______________ a little bit taller than me. (is)

   e) They _______________ a quarter and two dimes on the sidewalk. (find)

   f) She _______________ her teeth after each meal. (brush)

   © Chalkboard Publishing

4. Write the correct **present tense** form of the **helping verb** in brackets.

a) The waves __________ crashing on the shore. (be)

b) He __________ helping Mom paint the kitchen. (be)

c) I __________ sweeping up the crumbs on the floor. (be)

d) We __________ hoping the sun will come out soon. (be)

5. Rewrite each sentence to show the action happening in the **future**.

a) The hungry lions hunt for food.

____

b) I walk to the grocery store.

____

6. Circle the correct **helping verb** in brackets to tell about an action that has **already happened**.

a) The loud thunder (was   were   is) scaring the little children.

b) I (had   has) written my name at the top of the quiz.

c) The snowflakes (are   were   was) melting on my face.

d) She (have   has) promised to help me.

e) Our neighbors (have   has) invited us to a barbecue.

f) They (is   was   were) whispering secrets to each other.

Some Adverbs Describe How

An **adverb** describes a verb. An adverb can describe **how, when**, **where**, or **how often** an action happens.

On this page, you will work with adverbs that describe **how** an action happens.

Example: Tara quickly tied her shoes.

The adverb *quickly* describes **how** Tara tied her shoes.

In the example above, the adverb comes **before** the verb it describes. An adverb can also come **after** the verb it describes.

Examples: The woman spoke <u>softly</u>.   Eric ran up the steps <u>quickly</u>.

1. Underline the **adverb** that tells **how** an action happens.

   a) Fred slowly walked home.

   b) She quietly left the room.

   c) Carmella loudly shouted the answer.

   d) The boys carefully washed the glasses.

   e) The students correctly answered all of the questions.

   f) The father gently held his baby daughter.

2. Underline the **adverb** that tells **how** an action happens.

   a) The ballerina danced gracefully across the stage.

   b) The painters hummed happily as they worked.

   c) Leon answered the questions honestly.

   d) The grandmother smiled sweetly at her grandson.

   e) Susan held the baseball bat tightly.

   f) The thief tiptoed silently from the room.

© Chalkboard Publishing

Some Adverbs Describe When

An **adverb** describes a verb. An adverb can describe **how, when**, **where,** or **how often** an action happens.

On this page, you will work with **adverbs** that describe **when** an action happens.

Example: Cathy will visit us <u>tomorrow</u>.

The adverb *tomorrow* describes **when** Cathy will visit.

1. Underline only the adverbs that tell **when** an action happens.

   a) The children played noisily in the park this afternoon.

   b) Maggie will read her story next.

   c) Tomorrow, Alfredo will make a special dinner.

   d) Please close the window now.

   e) The rain will stop soon.

   f) The girls quickly cleaned up the mess at lunchtime.

   g) Yesterday, the dentist checked my teeth.

   h) Next, I will show you an amazing magic trick.

   i) The fire alarm rang, so Fernando left the building immediately.

2. Read each sentence and underline the **adverb.** Then complete the next sentence.

   a) Later, we will sing a song.

   The adverb _____________ tells **when** the action ___________ happens.

   b) Walt will swim next.

   The adverb _____________ tells **when** the action _____________ happens.

   c) Soon my friend will arrive.

   The adverb _____________ tells **when** the action _____________ happens.

Some Adverbs Describe Where

An **adverb** describes a verb. An adverb can describe **how, when**, **where**, or **how often** an action happens.

On this page, you will work with **adverbs** that describe **where** an action happens.

Example: Eddie and Tyler look <u>outside</u>.

The adverb *outside* describes **where** Eddie and Tyler look.

Some **adverbs** describe **where** something happens, but they **do not** describe the **exact place**.

Example: Abdul hid his book <u>somewhere</u>.

The adverb *somewhere* describes **where** Abdul hid his book.

1. Read the sentence and underline the **adverb**. Then complete the next sentence.

   a) I hang the picture here.

   The adverb _____________ tells **where** the action _____________ happens.

   b) Penny plays inside on rainy days.

   The adverb _____________ tells **where** the action _____________ happens.

   c) My brother found his book downstairs.

   The adverb _____________ tells **where** the action _____________ happens.

   d) They put the flowers there.

   The adverb _____________ tells **where** the action _____________ happens.

2. Underline the adverb that tells **where** an action happens.

   a) I searched everywhere for my umbrella.

   b) The frightened bird flew away.

   c) A lion roared nearby.

   d) You can put your coats anywhere.

   e) They hid the treasure somewhere.

© Chalkboard Publishing

Some Adverbs Describe How Often

An **adverb** describes a verb. An adverb can describe **how, when**, **where,** or **how often** an action happens.

On this page, you will work with **adverbs** that describe **how often** an action happens.

Example: They <u>sometimes</u> go camping in August.

The adverb **sometimes** describes **how often** they go camping in August.

Learn these **adverbs** that describe **how often** an action happens.

constantly (all the time)	**occasionally** (once in a while)
frequently (very often)	**seldom** (not very often)
usually (most of the time)	**rarely** (almost never)

1. Underline the adverb that tells **how often** an action happens.

   a) My neighbor always waves at me.

   b) Molly rang the doorbell twice.

   c) Mr. Cortez often hums his favorite song.

   d) My baby sister never cries.

   e) I flew on an airplane once.

2. In the **second** sentence, write one of the **adverbs** from the list above. Choose an adverb that **means the same** as the underlined words.

   a) Sam eats yogurt <u>very often</u>.   Sam _______________________ eats yogurt.

   b) The baby cries <u>all the time</u>.   The baby cries _______________________.

   c) I <u>almost never</u> catch a cold.   I _______________________ catch a cold.

   d) It rains <u>most of the time</u>.   It _______________________ rains.

   e) He dreams <u>not very often</u>.   He _______________________ dreams.

   f) You sneeze <u>once in a while</u>.   You sneeze _______________________.

Adverbs Review Quiz

1. The **adverbs** in the sentences below describe **how** an action happens. Circle the adverbs.

   a) The salesperson cheerfully asked if I needed any help.

   b) The man yelled angrily at the raccoons in his garden.

   c) This student has correctly answered all the questions.

   d) Carol gently put the crying baby in the crib.

   e) Ivan politely asked if he could join our game of hide-and-seek.

   f) The children had safely crossed the street when the light turned red.

   g) If you want to tell me a secret, whisper it quietly in my ear.

2. The **adverbs** in the sentences below describe **when** an action happens. Circle the adverbs.

   a) It snowed yesterday, and we made snowmen in the park.

   b) Mom is busy, but she will call you later.

   c) I am sure the bus will come soon.

   d) If the children are hungry, we can eat lunch now.

   e) Leon is happy that the sun is shining today.

   f) Rachel is taking her turn, and Roger will go next.

   g) Mr. and Mrs. Gallo will fly to France tomorrow.

   h) Dad left for work late.

© Chalkboard Publishing

Adverbs Review Quiz (continued)

3. The **adverbs** in the sentences below describe **where** an action happens. Circle the adverbs.

   a) Let us wait here and see if the rain stops.

   b) Mom went downstairs to answer the door.

   c) I think I left my keys somewhere in the living room.

   d) The women sat outside to enjoy the sunshine.

4. The **adverbs** in the sentences below describe **how often** an action happens. Circle the adverbs.

   a) Mrs. Kirby always feeds her cat in the morning.

   b) Joel often wins when I play checkers with him.

   c) I never cross the street before I look both ways.

   d) She called them twice, but no one answered the phone.

5. Circle the correct word to tell what the bold **adverb** describes.

   a) My sister touched me **lightly** on the shoulder.
      The adverb *lightly* describes (how   when   where   how often).

   b) Water the plant **weekly,** or the soil will dry out.
      The adverb *weekly* describes (how   when   where   how often).

   c) Melissa is not hungry, so she will eat **later**.
      The adverb *later* describes (how   when   where   how often).

   d) We stayed **inside** because the day was so cold.
      The adverb *inside* describes (how   when   where   how often).

Complete Subjects

There are two parts to a sentence. These parts are called the **complete subject** and the **complete predicate**. We will talk about complete predicates in another lesson.

The **complete subject** contains all the words that tell **who or what** the sentence is about. In the examples below, the complete subject is in bold.

Example: **The tiny black kitten** *snuggled beside its mother.*

This sentence is about a kitten. The complete subject contains **all** the words that tell about the kitten.

Example: **The bright lightning** *lit up the night sky.*

This sentence is about lightening. The complete subject contains **all** the words that tell about the lightening.

In each sentence, underline all the words in the **complete subject**.

a) The sly fox snuck into the hen house.

b) Several silly clowns were lined up for the parade.

c) Many different types of seashells were found onshore.

d) The lights of the city twinkled down below.

e) A large black bear wandered through our campsite.

f) My friend Jessica played an apple tree in our school play.

g) Many children in my class wear glasses.

h) The people of the town held a strawberry festival.

i) Fire trucks and firefighters rushed to put out the fire.

© Chalkboard Publishing

Complete Predicates

In a previous lesson, we talked about complete subject of a sentence, which tells who or what the sentence is about. Now we will talk about the rest of the sentence: The **complete predicate**.

The **complete predicate** includes the **verb** and **all** the words that tell about what happened in the sentence. In the examples below, the complete predicate is underlined.

Example: The forest fire <u>crept closer to the town</u>.

The verb in this sentence is *crept*. The other underlined words help to tell about what happened in the sentence.

Example: The ocean waves <u>washed the children's sand castle away</u>.

The verb in this sentence is *washed*. The other underlined words help to tell about what happened in the sentence.

Every word in a sentence will be part the complete subject **or** part of the complete predicate. In the examples below, the complete subject is in bold, and the complete predicate is underlined.

Examples: **The happy puppies** <u>chased a ball in our backyard</u>.
        Hens with red feathers <u>lay brown eggs.</u>.

In each sentence, underline all the words in the **complete predicate**.

a) A little green duck swims in our pool every day.

b) Little red beetles ate all my mother's lilies.

c) Seven brown puppies tumbled out of the box.

d) My sister and I made peanut butter sandwiches.

e) Some people read newspapers only on weekends.

f) My parents painted my bedroom mint green today.

g) This week's math homework contains multiplication problems.

h) The striped rubber ball rolled all the way down the hill.

What Comes at the End of a Sentence?

Put a **period** at the end of a **telling sentence**.

Example: We are going to the park.

Put a **question mark** at the end of a **question sentence**.

Example: Did you bring your umbrella?

Put an **exclamation mark** at the end of a sentence that shows a **strong feeling**. Anger, happiness, and excitement are examples of strong feelings.

Examples: You hurt me!   This is fun!   I can't wait!

Put a **period** or an **exclamation mark** at the end of a **command** sentence.

A **command** sentence tells someone to do something.

Examples: Hang your coat up.   Watch out!

1. Write the correct punctuation mark at the end of each sentence.

a) Would you like a slice of pizza____

b) Stop making so much noise____

c) Hooray, we are going to the zoo____

d) Are you going to the library____

e) The girls are watching the parade____

f) Be careful____

g) What is your favorite season of the year____

© Chalkboard Publishing

2. Write two examples of each kind of sentence. Be sure to include the correct punctuation at the end of each sentence.

a) Telling sentence:

____

____

____

b) Asking sentence:

____

____

____

c) Sentence that shows strong feeling:

____

____

____

d) Command sentence:

____

____

One Sentence or Two?

A short sentence usually tells **one idea**.

Examples: My mother lost her ring. (one idea)

I found it in the bathroom. (one idea)

Be careful when you write sentences. Check to see if you need to turn one sentence into two sentences.

*Example: This is **not** correct: I saw a puppy it was lost.*

*This is **correct**: I saw a puppy. It was lost.*

The sentences below are **not** correct. Correct each sentence by writing it as **two sentences**.

a) I like Lisa she is my friend.

____

b) Pak likes to run he runs fast.

____

c) It was raining I got wet.

____

d) Dad read a story it was funny.

____

e) The telephone rang it woke me up.

____

Remember to check your writing. Did you start each sentence with a capital letter?

© Chalkboard Publishing

Joining Sentences with *And* or *But*

You can use *and* to join together two short sentences.

Example: John bought crayons. He drew pictures.
John bought crayons, and he drew pictures.

You can also use *but* to join together short sentences. Use *but* when the idea in the
second sentence **goes against** the idea in the **first** sentence.

Example: Donna wants to stay up late. Her mom said no.
Donna wants to stay up late, but her mom said no.

1. Read the two sentences. Then use *and* or *but* to **join together** the two sentences.
   Write the **best word** to join the sentences.

   a) Carlos wanted to swim. He forgot his bathing suit.

   Carlos wanted to swim, __________ he forgot his bathing suit.

   b) She washes the dishes. I dry them

   She washes the dishes, __________ I dry them.

   c) Norma was not hungry. She ate a salad.

   Norma was not hungry, __________ she ate a salad.

   d) I like the zoo. We are going there tomorrow.

   I like the zoo, __________ we are going there tomorrow.

2. Each sentence below was made by joining together two short sentences. Complete
   each sentence by writing the joining word *and* or *but*. Put a comma **before** the
   joining word.

   a) The sun is shining ____________ it is a nice day.

   b) Hans watered the plant ____________ it died.

   c) I wore a warm coat ____________ I was still cold.

   d) Jana likes reading ____________ she reads often.

   e) Dad found his glasses ____________ he lost them again.

Joining Sentences with *Or* or *So*

You can use *or* to join together two short sentences. Use *or* when each sentence tells about two **different** actions, and only **one** action will happen.

Example: We can eat spaghetti for dinner tonight. We can eat chicken.
We can eat spaghetti for dinner tonight, or we can eat chicken.

You can use *so* to join together two short sentences. Use *so* when the idea in the **second** sentence happens **because of** the idea in the **first** sentence.

Example: It was raining. I took my umbrella.
It was raining, so I took my umbrella.

1. Write *or* or *so* to join together the sentences.

   a) We could walk to the park. We could ride our bikes there.

   We could walk to the park, ___________ we could ride our bikes there.

   b) Tina might arrive on time. She might be late.

   Tina might arrive on time, ___________ she might be late.

   c) My feet got wet. I dried them.

   My feet got wet, ___________ I dried them.

   d) Raj was hungry. He ate a snack.

   Raj was hungry, ___________ he ate a snack.

2. The sentences below were made by joining together two short sentences. Write the joining word *or* or *so*. Put a comma **before** the joining word.

   a) Her bike had a flat tire ___________ she walked to school.

   b) I might keep this photo ___________ I might give it to Stanley.

   c) Sandra might keep her hair long ___________ she might get it cut short.

   d) Mika had dirty hands ___________ he washed them.

© Chalkboard Publishing

Sentences and Punctuation Review Quiz

1. Add the correct **punctuation mark** (period, exclamation mark, or question mark) at the end of the sentence. Then tell **what kind** of sentence it is (telling, question, strong feeling, or command).

   a) I love my kitten so much   _______________________

   b) Tigers and zebras have stripes   _______________________

   c) Speak louder so we can hear you   _______________________

   d) Why did they leave so soon   _______________________

   e) A rainbow appeared in the sky   _______________________

   f) Is Hernando sick today   _______________________

2. If the sentence should be **two** sentences, **rewrite** it as two sentences. If the sentence is **correct** as one sentence, write "Correct."

   a) Tina is funny she makes me laugh.

   ____

   b) The birds ate seeds at the feeder.

   ____

   c) The sun was shining it was a nice day.

   ____

   d) The dogs are barking they make lots of noise.

   ____

3. Use the correct joining word (**and** or **but**) to join the sentences. Remember to add a **comma** before the joining word.

a) Alan plays piano. He practices every day.

____

b) I was tired. I did not go to bed.

____

c) Laura does not like grapes. She ate two anyway.

____

d) The phone rang. Dad answered it.

____

e) Wayne looks sick. He said he feels fine.

____

4. Circle the correct **joining word** in each sentence.

a) The movie was boring, (or   so) we played a video game instead.

b) It might snow tonight, (or   so) it might rain.

c) We had read the newspapers, (or   so) we put them in the recycling bin.

d) The computer was not working, (or   so) we asked Mom to fix it.

e) We could make dinner, (or   so) we could eat at a restaurant.

© Chalkboard Publishing

What Is a Contraction?

A **contraction** is one word made from two words, with one or more of the letters **left out**. The letters that are left out are replaced by an **apostrophe** ('). Look at the examples below.

Two Words	Contraction
I am	*I'm*
you are	*you're*
he is	*he's*
she is	*she's*

Two Words	Contraction
it is	*it's*
that is	*that's*
we are	*we're*
they are	*they're*

1. In each sentence, write the **contraction** for the words in brackets.

   a) They told me that _______________ telling the truth. (they are)

   b) _______________ the youngest child in my family. (I am)

   c) _______________ moving to a new house next month. (We are)

   d) Do you know that _______________ my best friend? (you are)

   e) _______________ my birthday today. (It is)

   f) Mom thinks _______________ the funniest joke she ever heard. (that is)

2. Rewrite each sentence. Use **contractions** for the underlined words.

   a) <u>She is</u> going to be upset if <u>he is</u> late.

   ____

   b) <u>I am</u> sure <u>that is</u> my notebook.

   ____

© Chalkboard Publishing

More Contractions

A **contraction** is one word made from two words, with one or more of the letters **left out**. The letters that are left out are replaced by an **apostrophe** ('). Below are some examples of contractions made with the word *will*.

Two Words	Contraction
I will	*I'll*
you will	*you'll*
he will	*he'll*

Two Words	Contraction
she will	*she'll*
we will	*we'll*
they will	*they'll*

1. In each sentence, write the **contraction** for the words in brackets.

   a) _____________ play baseball after school today. (We will)

   b) I hope _____________ feel better tomorrow. (you will)

   c) I wonder if _____________ help me find my mittens. (she will)

   d) _____________ wait for you on the playground. (I will)

   e) _____________ come to visit us next week. (They will)

   f) Do you think _____________ win the race? (he will)

2. Rewrite the sentences below. Write each **contraction** as two words.

   a) I'll bring sandwiches, and you'll bring juice. We'll have a great picnic!

   ____

   ____

   ____

© Chalkboard Publishing

Abbreviations

An **abbreviation** is the **short form** of a word. An abbreviation ends with a **period**. The abbreviations in the sentence below are in bold.

*Example: **Mrs.** Lopez drove **Mr.** Rogers to the store.*

Mrs. is the abbreviation of **mistress**, and **Mr.** is the abbreviation of **mister**.

Below are two abbreviations you probably have seen before.

*Example: **Dr.** Rashad lives at 32 King **St.***

Dr. is the abbreviation of **doctor**, and **St.** is the abbreviation of **street**.

Use **Dr.** only before someone's name. Look at the examples below.

*Example: I am going to see **Dr.** Johnson tomorrow.*

Dr. comes before the last name *Johnson*, so it is correct to use the abbreviation of **doctor**.

*Example: A **doctor** lives next door to us.*

In this sentence, **doctor** does **not** come before someone's name, so it would **not** be correct to use the abbreviation **Dr.**

Use **St.** only when it comes after the **name** of a street.

*Example: Carrie lives at 56 Forest **St.***

St. comes after the name of a street, so it is correct to use the abbreviation.

*Example: I live on a **street** that is close to the hospital.*

Street does **not** come after the name of a street, so it would **not** be correct to use the abbreviation in this sentence.

Below are two more abbreviations you see in addresses. Like **St.**, use these abbreviations **only** when they come after a name.

Word	Abbreviation	Example
avenue	Ave.	We are moving to 27 River **Ave.**
road	Rd.	The library is on Poplar **Rd.**

1. Circle the **correct choice** in brackets.

a) I have an appointment to see (doctor Dr.) Harris tomorrow.

b) We drove down a long and bumpy (road Rd.) to get there.

c) Turn left when you get to Pine (street St.) and you'll see the hospital.

d) They saw a long (avenue Ave.) with big trees on both sides.

e) Is (doctor Dr.) Rosco the only (doctor Dr.) in the hospital right now?

f) On Kingston (road Rd.), there are many new apartment buildings.

g) Did you forget which (street St.) I live on?

h) The school on Elm (avenue Ave.) has a large playground.

2. Rewrite the sentences below to show the proper use of **abbreviations**.

a) Doctor Grayson went to school with Mrs Scott.

____

b) Wilson ave. is near Westside Park.

____

c) How close is Tower Rd to the office where mr. Patel works?

____

d) Are there lots of trees on your st.?

____

© Chalkboard Publishing

Contractions and Abbreviations Review Quiz

1. In each sentence, write the **contraction** for the words in brackets.

a) I am sure that ___________ telling the truth. (he is)

b) Do you think ___________ going to be windy today? (it is)

c) ___________ finish painting this room tomorrow. (We will)

d) It might rain, so ___________ take my umbrella with me. (I will)

e) ___________ the funniest thing I have ever heard! (That is)

f) When will you know if ___________ be able to come? (you will)

g) ___________ still sleeping, so please be quiet. (They are)

2. In each sentence, write the **two words** for the contraction in brackets.

a) We do not think ________________ mind if we are a bit late. (she'll)

b) I really like these pants ________________ wearing today. (I'm)

c) ________________ going to go skating after lunch. (We're)

d) There are two eggs in the nest, and ________________ hatch very soon. (they'll)

e) I think ________________ going to win the game. (you're)

f) ________________ making cookies to sell at the bake sale. (She's)

g) I am sure ________________ help carry the boxes. (he'll)

h) ________________ be happy when they hear the good news. (They'll)

3. Write the **abbreviation** for the word in brackets.

   a) We saw ____________ Tanaka at the grocery store. (Doctor)

   b) I saw ____________ Gordon jogging in the park. (Mister)

   c) They rode their bikes down the hill on Lakeside ____________ (Avenue).

   d) My aunt lived on Forest ____________ before she moved. (Road)

4. Rewrite each sentence to correct any errors. Check to see if **abbreviations** and **contractions** are used correctly.

   a) Your going to be taller than you're father.

   ____

   b) Mrs Henderson thinks thats a wonderful idea.

   ____

   c) Hes certain that Alfonso lives on this St.

   ____

   d) Their walking they're dog along Wilson Rd.

   ____

   e) Western Ave is closed because its flooded.

   ____

© Chalkboard Publishing

Using *To*, *Too*, or *Two*

The word *to* can be used in different ways.

You can use *to* before a verb.
*Example: I like **to** swim.*

To can show where someone or something is going.
*Examples: I am walking **to** school.   She is giving the book **to** Carlos.*

The word *too* can be used in different ways.

Too can mean *also*.
*Example: Bob sings, and Anna sings, **too**.*

Too can mean *too much*.
*Example: It is **too** hot in here.*

The word *two* means the number *2*.

1. Complete each sentence by writing **to** or **too**.

a) Mom will drive us __________ the park.

b) I found a dime, and I found a quarter, __________.

c) I like __________ ride my new bike.

d) The soup is __________ hot to eat.

e) Terry is going __________ jump over the log.

f) Leon was hungry, and Akira was hungry, __________.

2. Write **to**, **too**, or **two** in the correct place in each sentence.

a) I am going __________ eat __________ muffins.

b) They are __________ tired __________ play __________ games of soccer.

c) She gave __________ apples __________ the children.

d) We saw __________ squirrels, and we saw __________ frogs, __________.

Write the Correct Word

The pairs of words below **sound the same** but are **spelled differently**. Make sure you write the word you mean.

Words	Examples
here – a place	Put your coat **here**.
hear – what your ears do	I can **hear** birds chirping.
see – what your eyes do	I **see** clouds in the sky.
sea – an ocean	The ship sailed across the **sea**.
right – correct, or the opposite of left	That is the **right** answer. I hurt my **right** foot.
write – make words on paper	She is going to **write** a story.

Circle the **correct word** in the brackets.

a) I know the (right   write) answer to the next question.

b) The (see   sea) had big waves during the storm.

c) The man told us to turn (right   write) at the next corner.

d) Do not leave your wet boots (here   hear).

e) My little brother can (right   write) his name.

f) Did you (see   sea) the rainbow this morning?

g) I could not (here   hear) what she said.

h) You were (right   write) when you said to turn (right   write).

i) We can (see   sea) the (see   sea) from (here   hear).

© Chalkboard Publishing

Correcting Errors: "The Lost Mitten"

Find and correct **eight** errors in the story below.

I could not find one of my blue mittens. I asked my brother and my sister. I asked my parents. No one had seen my mitten. Where was it.

I looked all over the house. I looked in my bedroom. I looked in my sisters bedroom. I looked in the kitchen and the living room, to. I could not find it. The blue mitten was lost.

I felt sad I loved my blue mittens. I had too other pairs of mittens, but the blue mittens were the warmer. I put on my green mittens. Then I went to say goodbye to our cat. I always say goodbye to freddy before I go to school.

Freddy was asleep on a chair. Can you guess what I found under Freddys' paw?

I found my blue mitten!

Correcting Errors: "Owls"

Find and correct **ten** errors in the article below.

1 Owls are big birds. An owls feathers can be gray, brown, or white. You can find owls in the United states, canada, and many other countries around the world.

2 Have you ever seen an owl. You will not see an owl during the day. Thats because owls sleep during the day. They wake up to hunt at night.

3 Owls are good hunters they can here very soft sounds. Owls have large eyes that can sea at night, and they have strong, sharp claws, two. Owls hunt frogs, mouses, bugs, and birds.

© Chalkboard Publishing

Vocabulary List 1

---

resident

(*noun*) someone who lives in a certain place or building

*Example: I know many of the **residents** in my apartment building.*

---

convince

(*verb*) to make someone believe that something is true, or to make someone agree to do something

*Examples: I **convinced** Leo that my pet snake will not bite him.*
*I will **convince** Tammy to lend me her bike.*

---

ancient

(*adjective*) very old, or from a time that was long ago

*Example: This **ancient** coin was made 1,000 years ago.*

---

purpose

(*noun*) the reason for doing something

*Example: Our **purpose** for cleaning out the basement was to get rid of things we do not need anymore.*

---

recall

(*verb*) to remember something

*Example: I know that woman, but I cannot **recall** where I met her.*

In each sentence, write the **correct word** from the vocabulary list. For **verbs**, remember to use the correct **form** and **tense** (past, present, or future).

a) Janelle thought I was lying, so I _____________________ her that I was telling the truth.

b) Discovering new lands was the _____________________ of the explorers' journey.

c) I now live in Alberta, so I am not a _____________________ of Manitoba anymore.

d) I wish I could _____________________ the name of the restaurant where we ate last week.

e) The scientists were excited to find _____________________ dinosaur bones buried underground.

f) We tried to _____________________ Mom to let us stay up late so we could watch the rest of the movie.

g) One _____________________ in our apartment building always climbs the stairs instead of using the elevator.

h) The _____________________ of wearing mittens or gloves is to keep your hands warm.

i) Do you _____________________ that time when we rode on the roller coaster at the amusement park?

j) If you would like to come to the museum with us, we can see many

_____________________ objects.

© Chalkboard Publishing

Vocabulary List 1: Review

Vocabulary words: resident   convince   ancient   purpose   recall

1. Write the correct **vocabulary word** beside each definition.

   a) _____________________: the reason for doing something

   b) _____________________: to make someone agree to do something

   c) _____________________: someone who lives in a certain place or building

   d) _____________________: very old, or from a time that was long ago

   e) _____________________: to remember something

2. Write the **correct** vocabulary word in each sentence. For **verbs**, remember to use the correct **form** and **tense** (past, present, or future).

   a) The _____________________ of wearing sunscreen is to make sure you do not get a sunburn.

   b) Yesterday, I _____________________ where I had put my book about secret codes.

   c) Jake is a great pitcher, so I am glad you _____________________ him to join our baseball team.

   d) When I was a _____________________ of this apartment building, I lived on the third floor.

   e) My parents thought I was too young to look after a puppy, so I had to

   _____________________ them I could do it.

   f) This _____________________ bowl was made 2,000 years ago.

Vocabulary List 2

---

vehicle

(*noun*) a machine that carries people or things from one place to another

*Example: Cars, trucks, buses, and motorcycles are examples of **vehicles**.*

---

observe

(*verb*) to carefully watch (and sometimes listen to)

*Example: The scientist will **observe** the birds to see how they build their nest.*

---

predict

(*verb*) to say or think what will happen in the future

*Example: I see dark clouds in the sky, so I **predict** it will rain soon.*

---

annual

(*adjective*) happening once a year

*Example: Our city's **annual** winter festival happens every January.*

---

signal

(*noun*) something such as a body movement, light, or sound that sends a message

*Example: The sound of the fire alarm is a **signal** that you should leave the building.*

(*verb*) to send a message by using a body movement, light, or sound

*Example: A red traffic light **signals** drivers that they need to stop.*

© Chalkboard Publishing

In each sentence, write the **correct word** from the vocabulary list. For **verbs**, remember to use the correct **form** and **tense** (past, present, or future).

a) A fire truck's siren is a _____________________ that drivers need to pull over to the side of the road.

b) At the magic show yesterday, I _____________________ the magician to see if I could find out how he did his tricks.

c) Someone who has a _____________________ large enough for seven people will give us a ride to the zoo.

d) Every July, we go to Chicago for our _____________________ visit with Uncle Frank and Aunt Judy.

e) Our team is three goals ahead, so I _____________________ that we will win the game.

f) The traffic lights are broken, so a police officer _____________________ to cars when they should go or stop.

g) A motorcycle is a _____________________ that can carry only one or two people.

h) I _____________________ that my parents will give me a new baseball glove for my birthday because they know I need one.

i) When the coach blows her whistle, it's a _____________________ that we should stop and listen to what she has to say.

j) For a week, the detective _____________________ the woman to find out where she went.

k) Your birthday is an _____________________ event.

Vocabulary List 2: Review

Vocabulary words: vehicle   observe   predict   annual   signal

1. Write the correct **vocabulary word** beside each definition.

   a) _____________________: something such as a body movement, light, or
   sound that sends a message

   b) _____________________: happening once a year

   c) _____________________: a machine that carries people or things from
   one place to another

   d) _____________________: to say or think what will happen in the future

   e) _____________________: to send a message by using a body
   movement, light, or sound

   f) _____________________: to carefully watch (and sometimes listen to)

2. Write the **correct** vocabulary word in each sentence. For **verbs**, remember to use
   the correct **form** and **tense** (past, present, or future).

   a) I studied hard for the test, so I _____________________ that I will get a good
   mark.

   b) A bus is a _____________________ that can carry a large number of people.

   c) We go on our _____________________ family vacation every August.

   d) Students usually raise their hand to _____________________ that they have a
   question.

   e) The parents _____________________ their children to make sure they took turns
   playing on the swings.

   f) The beeping of my alarm clock is a _____________________ that it is time to get
   up.

© Chalkboard Publishing

device

(*noun*) something that has been made to do a certain job

*Example: A shovel is a **device** people use to move dirt and snow.*

prevent

(*verb*) to stop something from happening

*Example: Putting on sunscreen can **prevent** you from getting a sunburn.*

attempt

(*noun*) a try at doing something

*Example: The batter's first **attempt** to hit the baseball was a strike.*

(*verb*) to try to do something

*Example: This box might be too heavy for me, but I will **attempt** to lift it.*

actual

(*adjective*) real or correct

*Examples: This toy giraffe is much shorter than an **actual** giraffe.*
*I thought the time was 1:00 p.m., but the **actual** time was 1:30 p.m.*

rarely

(*adverb*) not very often

*Example: Where we live, it **rarely** snows in April.*

In each sentence, write the **correct word** from the vocabulary list. For **verbs**, remember to use the correct **form** and **tense** (past, present, or future).

a) I fell quite a few times because it was my first ___________________ at skating.

b) It ___________________ rains in the desert, so not many plants can grow there.

c) A nail clipper is a ___________________ that people use to cut their fingernails and toenails.

d) This movie about George Washington is based on ___________________ events that happened in his life.

e) A bicycle helmet can ___________________ you from hurting your head if you fall.

f) The cat ___________________ to catch the mouse, but the mouse was too fast.

g) Kate ___________________ reads poems because she likes reading stories better.

h) I thought the movie would be about an hour and a half long, but its

___________________ length was two hours.

i) We put a fence around the backyard to ___________________ our dog from running out into the street.

j) A smoke detector is a ___________________ that tells people a fire might have started.

© Chalkboard Publishing

Vocabulary List 3: Review

Vocabulary words: device   attempt   prevent   actual   rarely

1. Write the correct **vocabulary word** beside each definition.

a) ____________________: to try to do something

b) ____________________: not very often

c) ____________________: to stop something from happening

d) ____________________: something that has been made to do a certain job

e) ____________________: real or correct

f) ____________________: a try at doing something

2. Write the **correct** vocabulary word in each sentence. For **verbs**, remember to use the correct **form** and **tense** (past, present, or future).

a) An umbrella will ____________________ you from getting wet.

b) She did not get the basketball in the hoop the first time she tried, but the

ball did go in on her second ____________________.

c) A microwave is a ____________________ that heats food quickly.

d) It rained so much last summer that I ____________________ had to water the garden.

e) The museum has only a copy of the old treasure map because the

____________________ map got lost.

Vocabulary List 4

arrange

(*verb*) to put in a neat, attractive, or proper order; to organize or make plans for

*Example: My mother **arranged** the flowers nicely in the vase.*

---

brief

(*adjective*) lasting only a short time

*Example: The butterfly sat on my arm only for a **brief** moment.*

---

cling

(*verb*) to hold on tightly to something

*Example: Tree frogs have sticky pads on their feet that help them **cling** to surfaces.*

---

crumple

(*verb*) to crush something so it becomes wrinkled and creased

*Example: Max was unhappy with his story, so he **crumpled** it up and threw it out.*

---

gradual

(*adjective*) taking place or progressing slowly or by degrees

*Example: In spring, there is a **gradual** change as the trees and flowers start to grow.*

---

swift

(*adjective*) happening quickly or immediately

*Example: The **swift** squirrel snatched the peanut and raced away with it.*

(*adverb*) describing something that moves quickly

*Example: The river is **swiftly** moving above the falls.*

© Chalkboard Publishing

In each sentence, write the **correct word** from the vocabulary list. For **verbs**, remember to use the correct **form** and **tense** (past, present, or future).

a) The woman carefully placed her folded clothes in her suitcase, so they would not get

_______________________.

b) In one _______________ move, the dog knocked the cup of water off the table and all over the floor.

c) I wish I could get taller fast, but I know it is a very _________________ process.

d) Our cat got scared by the dog's sudden barking, so she is now _________________ to the curtains.

e) My grandmother always _________________ the candies on my cake to spell "Happy Birthday!"

f) The candle made a _________________ sputtering sound before the flame went out.

g) That young man _________________ served his customers at the restaurant.

h) The packing peanuts from the shipping box are _________________ to my cat's fur.

i) The change in the baby's eye color was so _________________ that we only saw the difference in photos.

j) The neighbor's dog stopped barking for one _________________ minute before he started all over again.

k) The scrap metal dealer _________________ to pick up the old rusty car.

Vocabulary List 4: Review

Vocabulary words: arrange brief cling crumple gradual swift

1. Write the correct **vocabulary word** beside each definition.

a) ________________________________: taking place or progressing slowly

b) ________________________________: happening quickly or immediately

c) ________________________________: to put in a neat, attractive, or proper order

d) ________________________________: to hold on tightly to something

e) ________________________________: to crush, crease, and wrinkle something

f) ________________________________: describing something that moves quickly

2. Write the **correct** vocabulary word in each sentence. For **verbs**, remember to use the correct **form** and **tense** (past, present, or future).

a) Many people complain that spring and summer are too ____________ in Canada.

b) After the accident, my uncle made ______________ progress in learning to walk again.

c) Our dog is very ____________ at escaping from my little brother's hugs.

d) I sat on my new dress the wrong way and the skirt part got all ________________.

e) Aunt Amy whispered that she is ______________ a party for my Uncle Ben for next weekend.

f) The kind knight was ______________ in moving to help the woman who had fallen.

 © Chalkboard Publishing

Vocabulary List 5

avoid

(*verb*) to keep away from something, or stop oneself from doing something

*Example: The traffic report warned people to **avoid** Mill Street because it was flooded.*

---

clever

(*adjective*) smart; quick to learn, understand, or come up with ideas

*Example: My teacher said my idea for a mouse maze was very **clever**.*

---

doze

(*verb*) to sleep lightly

*Example: My grandfather always **dozes** off while watching television.*

---

flutter

(*verb*) to fly unsteadily or hover by flapping wings quickly and lightly

*Example: The little bird **fluttered** its wings while trying to land on the swaying branch.*

---

marsh

(*noun*) an area of land that is always very wet; a wetland

*Example: Frogs, turtles, beavers, and muskrats live among the cattails in the **marsh**.*

---

risk

(*noun*) a situation involving exposure to danger

*Example: The thief took a big **risk** by trying to sneak past the sleeping dog.*

(*verb*) to expose someone or something to danger, harm, or loss

*Example: Jack **risked** dropping the glass when he picked it up with his wet hands.*

Vocabulary List 5 (continued)

In each sentence, write the **correct word** from the vocabulary list. For **verbs**, remember to use the correct **form** and **tense** (past, present, or future).

a) My uncle, my father, and I went to see the tadpoles in the ______________.

b) The old bridge is worn out, so you should not ______________ walking across it.

c) Our pet rat is very ______________. He has learned to do several tricks.

d) My baby sister is finally asleep, so we have to ______________ making too much noise.

e) The girl was relaxing in the hammock, and slowly ______________ off.

f) The butterfly was ______________ its wings as it tried to land on the flower.

g) The people urged the mayor to protect the ______________ where the ducks nest every year.

h) The girl took the __________ of hurting her feet when she wore flipflops on the hike.

i) My mother learned a ______________ new way of folding napkins to make swans.

j) My brother can be lazy sometimes. He often tries to ______________ doing his chores.

k) My cousin's cat ______________ on the window sill in the sunshine this morning.

© Chalkboard Publishing

Vocabulary List 5: Review

Vocabulary words: avoid clever doze flutter marsh risk

1. Write the correct **vocabulary word** beside each definition.

a) _________________________________: to fly unsteadily by flapping wings quickly

b) _________________________________: to keep away from something

c) _________________________________: a situation involving exposure to danger

d) _________________________________: an area of land that is always very wet

e) _________________________________: to sleep lightly

f) _________________________________: smart

g) _________________________________: to expose to danger

2. Write the **correct** vocabulary word in each sentence. For **verbs**, remember to use the correct **form** and **tense** (past, present, or future).

a) The bird _____________ its wings while it ate the baby spiders off the window.

b) I want to _____________ looking bad, so I will not cut my own hair.

c) On Saturdays, I often stay in bed late and _____________ a little longer.

d) Macy knew Robbie would tease her, so she _____________ him in at recess.

e) I found a _____________ new way to tie my shoelaces.

f) My brother took a _____________ and asked Cara to the dance.

g) The town held a weekend event to clean up the _____________.

© Chalkboard Publishing

1. Underline all the **nouns** in each sentence.

   a) The dog plays with the tennis ball in the park.

   b) Most children enjoy making paintings with their fingers.

   c) My uncle used a hammer and nails to fix the shed.

   d) Kittens and puppies are popular pets for families with children.

   e) Marco decided to play soccer instead of playing baseball.

2. Write the **plural** of each noun.

   a) bunch _______________   b) child _______________

   c) puppy _______________   d) zero _______________

   e) fox _______________   f) elf _______________

   g) potato _______________   h) photo _______________

   i) berry _______________   j) roof _______________

3. In each sentence, circle the correct **possessive noun**. Think about whether the sentence needs a **singular** or **plural** possessive noun.

   a) My (brothers'   brother's) bicycles are all too small for them now.

   b) The (officer's   officers') lights were flashing.

   c) My three (hamsters'   hamster's) favorite hiding place is this box.

   d) This (Sundays'   Sunday's) class was about being kind to others.

© Chalkboard Publishing

4. Rewrite each sentence. Use a **pronoun** to replace each **underlined word** or **group of words**.

a) Karen hopes that <u>Karen</u> can go camping with <u>her cousins</u> this summer.

____

b) <u>My family and I</u> are going to the zoo tomorrow with <u>my aunt</u>.

____

c) <u>The happy puppies</u> played with <u>the little boy</u>.

____

5. In each sentence, write the correct **possessive pronoun** to replace the word or words in brackets.

a) Ravi is moving to Oregon with _______________ family. (Ravi's)

b) _______________ note was taped to _______________ door. (Mom's; the fridge's)

c) The boys met __________ favorite baseball player. (the boys')

6. Rewrite each sentence. Replace the **underlined words** with a **possessive pronoun**.

a) <u>Her book is</u> heavier than <u>my book</u>.

____

b) <u>Your mittens</u> are more <u>colorful</u> than <u>their mittens</u>.

____

c) <u>The firefighters'</u> bell is as loud as <u>the church's</u> bell.

____

7. Circle each **adjective** and underline each **noun**. Draw an arrow from each **adjective** to the **noun** it describes.

a) I wanted to watch another movie, but everyone was tired.

b) Sonny barbecued delicious burgers for dinner.

c) The young squirrels are playful today.

d) Bright lightning lit up the stormy sky.

8. In each sentence, circle the correct way to use **adjectives** to compare.

a) All the men were strong, but Little Mike was (stronger   the strongest).

b) This tree is tall, but that tree is (taller   the tallest).

c) All the dogs at the dog show were pretty, but my dog is (prettier   the prettiest).

9. In each sentence, circle the correct way to **compare** two or more things.

a) Todd studied a lot, but his sister studied (more   the most).

b) Ana and Hans was tired after the hike, but Terry was (more   the most) tired.

c) Kai is (more   the most) flexible person in gymnastics class.

10. Complete the sentences with the correct word—*a*, *an*, or *the*.

a) __________ spider and __________ octopus look a bit alike.

b) In __________ store, we saw __________ ant farm.

c) If you cut __________ apple through the middle, you will see __________ star inside.

d) It is amazing how __________ cat and __________ dog are such good friends.

© Chalkboard Publishing

11. Circle all the **verbs** in each sentence.

   a) The players kicked and passed the soccer balls around the field.

   b) Mom and I mixed the cookie dough, then baked the cookies.

   c) We pulled the weeds, planted the flowers, then watered the garden.

   d) Making pizza and laughing with my family are two of my favorite activities.

12. Write the correct **present tense** form of the verb in brackets. (The present tense tells about actions that are happening **now**.)

   a) Yu __________ her bed every morning. (make)

   b) The baker __________ the dough to make the bread. (mix)

   c) A chick ___________ its way out of its shell. (peck)

13. Write the correct **past tense** form of the verb in brackets. (The past tense tells about actions that have **already happened**.)

   a) Ted _____________ his mother if Aaron could stay for dinner. (ask)

   b) My dad _____________ all the laundry this weekend. (wash)

   c) Rani _____________ some muffins at the school bake sale. (buy).

14. Write the correct **future tense** form of the verb in brackets. (The future tense tells about actions that will happen **in the future**.) Remember to use a **helping verb**.

   a) On Saturday, I _______________ to my cousin's party. (go)

   b) My brother and I _____________ some nice presents for our grandparents. (make)

   c) Katy and Tim _______________ to the store to buy bread. (walk)

   d) Mom __________________ my name in my jacket so I will not lose it. (stitch)

15. Circle the **linking** verbs and underline the **action** verbs.

a) I lost my dime, but I found a quarter.

b) We are all hungry for pizza.

c) This jacket is my favorite.

d) Kathy folded her paper and tucked it in her notebook.

16. Circle each **helping verb** and underline each **main verb**.

a) All of us are going to the fair this weekend.

b) My teacher will run in a marathon tomorrow.

c) My class is excited about the field trip.

d) When my dog is hungry, he drools.

17. Write the correct form of the **verb** in brackets. Make sure the subject and the verb **agree**.

a) The ponies _______________ around the field. (runs)

b) Kerry _______________ all the floors in the house. (sweep)

c) The sky turns dark and lightning _______________. (flash)

d) The bird _______________ to its nest. (fly)

e) The pink paper _______________ easier. (rip)

18. Circle the correct **helping verb** in brackets to tell about an action that has **already happened**.

a) My brother (was   is   were) helping my dad mow the lawn.

b) She (had   has) worked for most of her life.

c) Our cousins (is   are   were) all coming over for a barbecue today.

d) Those (are was   were) my favorite pair of jeans.

© Chalkboard Publishing

19. Circle the **adverbs** that describe **how**, **when**, **where**, **or how often** an action happens.

a) Mary always brushes her teeth after meals.

b) Theo takes out the garbage on Tuesdays.

c) The birds dropped seeds everywhere.

d) Victor shouted to Hans loudly.

e) Our uncle's dog rarely barks.

20. Add the correct **punctuation mark** (period, exclamation mark, or question mark) at the end of the sentence. Then tell **what kind** of sentence it is (telling, question, strong feeling, or command).

a) I can finally reach it____   ________________________________

b) I want to watch this____   ________________________________

c) Can you tell the time____   ________________________________

d) Marcel just came home____   ________________________________

e) Help me set the table____   ________________________________

21. In each sentence, write the **contraction** for the words in brackets.

a) ____________ sunny and hot out today. (It is)

b) ____________ hurt yourself if you jump that far. (You will)

c) I told my mother ____________ leaving for school now. (I am)

d) ____________ coming over this afternoon. (They are)

e) Kelly said ____________ going to move away soon. (she is)

____

NAME

Achievement Award – Grammar Practice Grade 3

____

NAME

110
© Chalkboard Publishing

Answers

What Is a Noun? p. 2

1. Tom, girl, man, Maria, grandfather, doctor

2. school, library, backyard, mall, beach, Michigan

3. lamp, pencil, coat, car, tree

4. a) shoe, carrot, basement **b)** teacher, bed **c)** baby, sister, bedroom

5. a) kitchen **b)** Carlos, street **c)** truck, house **d)** Mom, bathroom

6. Answers will vary. Ensure the sentence includes three nouns.

7. Answers will vary. Ensure the sentence includes a person and a place.

8. Answers will vary. Ensure the sentence includes a person, a place, and a thing.

Make a Noun Collage, p. 3

You may wish to make a bulletin board display of children's collages.

What Are Proper Nouns? p. 4

1. b) New Year's Day

Answers to all other questions on this page will vary. Ensure that proper nouns start with a capital letter.

Making Nouns Plural, p. 5

1. a) dishes **b)** bunnies **c)** bushes **d)** boxes **e)** wishes **f)** matches

2. a) I got scratches on my arms. **b)** I saw ladies wearing dresses.

Tricky Plural Nouns, pp. 6–8

1. a) patios **b)** zeros **c)** tomatoes **d)** pianos

2. a) The heroes turned on radios to hear the news. **b)** Larry sent me photos of potatoes from his garden. **c)** In the videos, people heard echoes.

3. a) halves **b)** thieves **c)** wolves **d)** shelves

4. a) The chefs made loaves of bread. **b)** Leaves blew onto the roofs. **c)** It is dangerous to play near cliffs. **d)** The sheriffs caught thieves.

5. a) knives **b)** fish **c)** lives **d)** sheep

6. a) The wives made lots of food for the party. **b)** Mice ran over my feet! **c)** The children fed the geese. **d)** The women saw deer in the woods.

Nouns Review Quiz, pp. 9–10

1. a) person, place, thing **b)** proper

2. a) Mom, mittens, shelf, closet **b)** Bees, butterflies, flowers, backyard **c)** mountains, Colorado **d)** nurse, doctor, papers **e)** windows, bird, house **f)** Darnell, beach, friends

3. a) Mrs. Greenway, Tuesday **b)** Rover, Maine **c)** Dr. Conway, Thanksgiving **d)** Chicago, United States **e)** Uncle Alfred, Florida **f)** Valentine's Day, February

4. a) boxes **b)** people **c)** videos **d)** lunches **e)** keys **f)** tomatoes **g)** babies **h)** wolves **i)** deer **j)** mice **k)** brushes **l)** shelves **m)** knives **n)** geese

5. a) sleeves **b)** videos **c)** children **d)** echoes **e)** roofs **f)** teeth **g)** tomatoes **h)** ponies

Singular Possessive Nouns, p. 11

1. a) Amira's b) bird's c) Omar's d) woman's

2. a) Mario turned the book's pages. b) The mug's handle broke off. c) The plant's leaves turned brown.

Plural Possessive Nouns, p. 12

1. a) sisters' b) cousins' c) cars' d) lions'

2. a) people's b) children's c) men's d) women's

More Practice with Possessive Nouns, pp. 13–14

1. a) My bike's front tire is flat. b) Please give me the store's phone number. c) Did you find Suki's pencil? d) This is my father's watch. e) The elephant's feet are huge!

2. a) The trees' leaves change color in the fall. b) The jars' lids are in the top drawer. c) The people's cars are parked outside. d) My brothers' coats are in the closet. e) We could hear the women's voices.

Possessive Nouns Review Quiz, pp. 15–16

1. a) shirt's b) puppies' c) children's d) Kim's e) shoes' f) team's g) Kayla's

2. a) Underline "plant's," cross it out, and write "plants' " above it. b) Underline "bird's" and put a check mark above it. c) Underline "Liams'," cross it out, and write "Liam's" above it. d) Underline "sister's," cross it out, and write "sisters' " above it. e) Underline "Jeremy's" and put a check mark above it; underline "coats'," cross it out, and write "coat's" above it. f) Underline "womens'," cross it out, and write "women's" above it; underline "men's" and put a check mark above it. g) Underline "markers' " and put a check mark above it.

3. a) aunt's b) monkey's c) dog's d) cat's e) Jim's f) girl's g) team's

4. a) children's b) Scouts' c) women's d) clouds' e) people's f) men's g) racers'

Pronouns for People, p. 17

1. a) He b) They c) them

2. a) They played with the puppies. b) She showed the picture to him. c) They smiled at us. d) We waved goodbye to them.

Pronouns for Things, p. 18

1. a) it b) They c) them d) They

2. a) They gave them to us. b) They are too big for them to carry. c) We sent it to him. d) Will they sing for them?

Possessive Pronouns, pp. 19–20

1. a) my b) his c) their d) your e) My, our f) its g) her h) Our, their

2. a) Frank scratched his nose because it was itchy. b) We are going to have dinner at her house. c) The Smiths saw birds eating from their bird feeder. d) Its batteries are dead. e) "Emilio, is it your birthday today?" Gary asked. f) The teachers said, "It is our job to help you learn." g) Gail said, "You can borrow my eraser." h) The toy truck is missing one of its wheels.

More Possessive Pronouns, p. 21

1. a) Underline "his"; circle "mine." b) Underline "her"; circle "his." c) Circle "Yours" and "hers." d) Underline "their"; circle "ours" and "theirs." e) Circle "Hers" and "his."

Question at bottom of page: The possessive pronoun "his" sometimes comes before a noun and sometimes does not in these questions. Look at sentences (a) and (b).

 © Chalkboard Publishing

2. a) My brother's feet are bigger than mine. **b)** Our dog barks louder than theirs. **c)** I think your joke is funnier than his. **d)** Are these hers or his?

3. a) our, theirs **b)** Your, mine **c)** My, yours **d)** ours **e)** mine, mine, hers **f)** your, theirs

Pronouns Review Quiz, pp. 23–24

1. a) My name is Eddie, and I can help you. **b)** We worked hard on our project. **c)** Please put them in the freezer. **d)** They gave him a birthday card. **e)** She has already returned them to us. **f)** They are too big for her. **g)** It is not too hard for them to read. **h)** He gave one apple to each of them.

2. a) His **b)** her, its **c)** their **d)** My **e)** Our **f)** Your **g)** their

3. a) Yours are longer than mine. **b)** His can jump farther than hers. **c)** Ours is on a higher floor than theirs. **d)** Hers is messier than mine.

What Is an Adjective? pp. 25–26

1. a) Circle "brown" and underline "mouse." **b)** Circle "large" and underline "book." **c)** Circle "scary" and underline "dragon." **d)** Circle "playful" and underline "puppy." **e)** Circle "green" and underline "mug." **f)** Circle "slippery" and underline "ice." **g)** Circle "loud" and underline "thunder." **h)** Circle "interesting" and underline "movie." **i)** Circle "funny" and underline "joke." **j)** Circle "round" and underline "table." **k)** Circle "tall" and underline "mountain." **l)** Circle "dirty" and underline "dishes." **m)** Circle "lonely" and underline "road." **n)** Circle "tall" and underline "grass." **o)** Circle "happy" and underline "dance." **p)** Circle "colorful" and underline "pigeons." **q)** Circle "angry" and underline "cat."

2. Sample answers: **a)** blue, new, warm **b)** loud, soft, clear **c)** dark, white, fluffy **d)** fast, quick, strong **e)** colorful, pretty, pink **f)** white, fat, hungry **g)** sleeping, lazy, tired

3. a) heavy **b)** warm **c)** bright **d)** great **e)** favorite **f)** sleepy, warm **g)** pretty, dark

Adjectives Before and After Nouns, p. 27

1. a) Circle "funny" and underline "clown." **b)** Circle "red" and underline "light." **c)** Circle "angry" and underline "woman." **d)** Circle "dry" and underline "towels." **e)** Circle "exciting" and underline "video." **f)** Circle "soft" and underline "pillow." **g)** Circle "cute" and underline "baby." **h)** Circle "delicious" and underline "sandwiches." **i)** Circle "bright" and underline "sun." **j)** Circle "cold" and underline "water." **k)** Circle "tired" and underline "Enzo." **l)** Circle "correct" and underline "answer."

2. a) Circle "huge" and underline "dinosaur"; draw an arrow from "huge" to "dinosaur." Circle "sharp" and underline "teeth"; draw an arrow from "sharp" to "teeth." **b)** Circle "happy" and underline "children"; draw an arrow from "happy" to "children." Circle "colorful" and underline "rainbow"; draw an arrow from "colorful" to "rainbow." **c)** Circle "tall" and underline "woman"; draw an arrow from "tall" to "woman." Circle "leaky" and underline "roof"; draw an arrow from "leaky" to "roof."

Adjectives Can Describe How Many, p. 28

1. a) Circle "three" and underline "apples"; draw an arrow from "three" to "apples." Underline "tree." **b)** Underline "Raj." Circle "four" and underline "coins"; draw an arrow from "four" to "coins." Underline "bed." **c)** Underline "Sandra." Circle "two" and underline "squirrels"; draw an arrow from "two" to "squirrels." Underline "tree." **d)** Circle "eight" and underline "frogs"; draw an arrow from "eight" to "frogs." Underline "pond."

2. a) several **b)** many **c)** Few **d)** some **e)** many, few **f)** several, many

Using Adjectives to Compare Two Things, p. 29

1. a) older **b)** thicker **c)** smaller **d)** colder **e)** brighter **f)** warmer **g)** softer

2. a) sadder **b)** hotter **c)** fatter **d)** bigger

Using Adjectives to Compare More Than Two Things, p. 30

1. a) fastest; runners in the race **b)** coldest; days of the year **c)** warmest; all the coats **d)** softest; all the beds

2. a) the cleanest **b)** the brightest **c)** the thickest **d)** the smallest

Tricky Adjectives That Compare, p. 31

a) better; two things **b)** worse; two things **c)** the best; more than two things **d)** farther; two things **e)** the most; more than two things **f)** the worst; more than two things

Adjectives That Use *More* and *Most* to Compare, p. 32

1. a) more **b)** the most **c)** more **d)** the most **e)** more **f)** the most **g)** more **h)** the most

2. a) grumpiest **b)** hairier **c)** sillier **d)** curliest

Make an Adjective Poem, p. 33

You may wish to create a bulletin board display of children's poems.

Using the Articles *A*, *An*, and *The*, pp. 34–35

a) the **b)** an **c)** the **d)** an **e)** The **f)** a, the **g)** an, a **h)** a, a **i)** a, an **j)** the, the **k)** The, a, the **l)** the, the **m)** A, the, an

Adjectives and Articles Review Quiz, pp. 36–37

1. a) Circle "old," underline "man," and draw an arrow from "old" to "man"; circle "big," underline "house," and draw an arrow from "big" to "house"; circle "beautiful," underline "lake," and draw an arrow from "beautiful" to "lake." **b)** Circle "wet," underline "floor," and draw an arrow from "wet" to "floor"; circle "slippery" and draw an arrow from "slippery" to "floor." **c)** Underline "soup," circle "hot," and draw an arrow from "hot" to "soup"; circle "delicious" and draw an arrow from "delicious" to "soup." **d)** Circle "Two," underline "women," and draw an arrow from "Two" to "women"; underline "chairs"; circle "tall," underline "tree," and draw an arrow from "tall" to "tree." **e)** Circle "Many," underline "children," and draw an arrow from "Many" to "children"; circle "funny," underline "stories," and draw an arrow from "funny" to "stories"; circle "scary," underline "stories," and draw an arrow from "scary" to "stories." **f)** Circle "Several," underline "people," and draw an arrow from "Several" to "people"; circle "some," underline "snacks," and draw an arrow from "some" to "snacks"; underline "party." **g)** Circle "Few," underline "guests," and draw an arrow from "Few" to "guests"; circle "four," underline "people," and draw an arrow from "four" to "people." **h)** Circle "little," underline "boy," and draw an arrow from "little" to "boy"; circle "red," underline "hair," and draw an arrow from "red" to "hair"; circle "tired" and draw an arrow from "tired" to "boy."

2. a) faster **b)** the loudest **c)** longer **d)** shorter **e)** the tallest **f)** the hungriest **g)** funnier

3. a) more **b)** the most **c)** the most **d)** more **e)** the most **f)** more

4. a) a **b)** the **c)** a **d)** an **e)** a **f)** the **g)** an

What Is a Verb? p. 38

1. a) jumps **b)** flies **c)** gives **d)** flashes **e)** forgets **f)** sends **g)** see **h)** squeaks **i)** dance **j)** runs

2. a) tells, cleans **b)** writes, says **c)** builds, explores **d)** hears, hides **e)** buys, pours **f)** remembers, asks, scrubs **g)** skips, decides

Make a Verb Collage, p. 39

You may wish to make a bulletin board display of children's collages.

© Chalkboard Publishing

The Verbs *Be*, *Do*, and *Have*, pp. 40–41
1. a) is **b)** are **c)** am **d)** are
2. a) do **b)** does **c)** do **d)** does
3. a) have **b)** have **c)** has **d)** have
4. a) was **b)** had **c)** did **d)** had **e)** were, was **f)** had
5. a) was **b)** did **c)** had **d)** were **e)** had **f)** were

More Practice with *Be*, *Do*, and *Have*, pp. 42–43
1. a) past **b)** present **c)** past **d)** past **e)** present **f)** present **g)** past **h)** present **i)** present
2. a) was **b)** have **c)** did **d)** were **e)** am **f)** have **g)** did
3. a) was **b)** did **c)** have **d)** are **e)** had **f)** did **g)** are **h)** did **i)** has

Linking Verbs, pp. 44–45
1. a) Circle "were." **b)** Underline "ran." **c)** Circle "is." **d)** Circle "are." **e)** Underline "fell." **f)** Circle "am."
2. a) Underline "painted" and circle "is." **b)** Circle "are" and underline "eat." **c)** Circle "were" and underline "picked."
   d) Circle "am" and underline "build." **e)** Circle "is" and "was." **f)** Underline "slipped" and "fell." **g)** Circle "were"
   and underline "laughed." **h)** Circle "are" and underline "drew." **i)** Underline "swam" and circle "was." **j)** Circle
   "am" and "is."

Spelling Present Tense Verbs, p. 46
1. a) copies **b)** cries **c)** buys **d)** flies **e)** tries
2. a) scratches **b)** pushes **c)** passes **d)** mixes **e)** catches

Past Tense Verbs, p. 47
1. a) invented **b)** coughed **c)** shared **d)** worked **e)** borrowed **f)** escaped **g)** agreed **h)** exploded
2. a) chased **b)** chewed **c)** filled
3. a) past **b)** present **c)** present

Spelling Past Tense Verbs, p. 48
1. a) tripped **b)** stopped **c)** stirred **d)** dripped **e)** stepped
2. a) cried **b)** carried **c)** hurried **d)** worried **e)** scurried

Tricky Past Tense Verbs, pp. 49–50
1. a) had **b)** said **c)** ate **d)** came
2. a) We drive to the grocery store. **b)** The squirrel eats all the nuts. **c)** I have two pencils in my desk. **d)** Carly
comes to my house every week.
3. a) went **b)** drank **c)** thought **d)** bought
4. a) We drink juice with our breakfast. **b)** He buys a new toy for his grandson. **c)** Anna finds lots of seashells at
   the beach. **d)** I think about my best friend.

Future Tense Verbs, p. 51
1. a) will ride **b)** will swim **c)** will shine **d)** will drive
2. a) Timothy will plant a tree in the backyard. **b)** Carlos and Mary will talk about the movie. **c)** People will laugh at
   all my silly jokes.

Helping Verbs: Present and Future Tenses, pp. 52–53

1. a) Circle "is" and underline "looking." **b)** Circle "is" and underline "blowing." **c)** Circle "am" and underline "brushing." **d)** Circle "are" and underline "chasing." **e)** Circle "is" and underline "cutting." **f)** Circle "am" and underline "working." **g)** Circle "are" and underline "pulling." **h)** Circle "are" and underline "washing."

2. a) The children will plant tulips. **b)** We will hang the pictures on the wall. **c)** I will sing my favorite song. **d)** The birds will build a nest in the tree. **e)** They will ask the librarian some questions.

Helping Verbs: Past Tense, pp. 54–55

1. a) Circle "has" and underline "walked." **b)** Circle "had" and underline "chewed." **c)** Circle "have" and underline "grown." **d)** Circle "have" and underline "dropped." **e)** Circle "has" and underline "dried." **f)** Circle "had" and underline "stopped." **g)** Circle "have" and underline "wrapped." **h)** Circle "have" and underline "played." **i)** Circle "have" and underline "built." **j)** Circle "has" and underline "invited." k) Circle "had" and underline "melted."

2. a) was **b)** were **c)** were **d)** was **e)** was **f)** were

3. a) walked **b)** chirping **c)** climbing **d)** stirring **e)** collecting

Subject–Verb Agreement, pp. 56–57

1. a) runs **b)** glows **c)** sail **d)** grow **e)** scratches **f)** wish **g)** follows **h)** blow

2. a) studies **b)** falls **c)** unload **d)** brushes **e)** bury **f)** look

3. a) rushes **b)** watches **c)** say **d)** jumps **e)** sing **f)** creeps **g)** goes **h)** ride **i)** hisses

Pronoun–Verb Agreement, pp. 58–59

1. a) matches **b)** see **c)** fixes **d)** run **e)** count **f)** finds **g)** lend

2. a) kisses **b)** tie **c)** makes **d)** takes **e)** touches **f)** notice **g)** chew **h)** misses

3. a) keeps; a blanket **b)** make; batteries **c)** buzzes; alarm clock **d)** help; glasses **e)** goes; belt **f)** come; firefighters

Verbs Review Quiz 1, pp. 60–61

1. a) grow, cut **b)** cheers, hits **c)** climb, pick **d)** erased, wrote

2. a) make, tell, takes **b)** find, ask, sees **c)** write, listen, bring

3. a) does **b)** fixes **c)** catch **d)** flies **e)** buys **f)** misses **g)** am

4. a) walked **b)** clapped **c)** was **d)** carried **e)** finished **f)** drove **g)** bought **h)** knew **i)** were

5. a) will call **b)** will read **c)** will visit **d)** will grow **e)** will make

Verbs Review 2, pp. 62–63

1. a) Circle "was" and underline "found." **b)** Underline "read" and circle "are." **c)** Circle "were" and underline "told." **d)** Circle "was" and "were."

2. a) Circle "is" and underline "making." **b)** Circle "were" and underline "honking." **c)** Circle "am" and underline "running." **d)** Circle "are" and underline "singing."

3. a) climb **b)** uses **c)** has **d)** are **e)** find **f)** brushes

4. a) are **b)** is **c)** am **d)** are

5. a) The hungry lions will hunt for food. **b)** I will walk to the grocery store.

6. a) was **b)** had **c)** were **d)** has **e)** have **f)** were

Some Adverbs Describe How, p. 64

1. a) slowly **b)** quietly **c)** loudly **d)** carefully **e)** correctly **f)** gently

2. a) gracefully **b)** happily **c)** honestly **d)** sweetly **e)** tightly **f)** silently

© Chalkboard Publishing

Some Adverbs Describe When, p. 65

1. a) this afternoon **b)** next **c)** Tomorrow **d)** now **e)** soon **f)** at lunchtime **g)** Yesterday **h)** Next **i)** immediately

2. a) Later; later, sing **b)** next; next, swim **c)** Soon; soon, arrive

Some Adverbs Describe Where, p. 66

1. a) here: here, hang **b)** inside; inside, plays **c)** downstairs; downstairs, found **d)** there; there, put

2. a) everywhere **b)** away **c)** nearby **d)** anywhere **e)** somewhere

Some Adverbs Describe How Often, p. 67

1. a) always **b)** twice **c)** often **d)** never **e)** once

2. a) frequently **b)** constantly **c)** rarely **d)** usually **e)** seldom **f)** occasionally

Adverbs Review Quiz, pp. 68–69

1. a) cheerfully **b)** angrily **c)** correctly **d)** gently **e)** politely **f)** safely **g)** quietly

2. a) yesterday **b)** later **c)** soon **d)** now **e)** today **f)** next **g)** tomorrow **h)** late

3. a) here **b)** downstairs **c)** somewhere **d)** outside

4. a) always **b)** often **c)** never **d)** twice

5. a) how **b)** how often **c)** when **d)** where

Complete Subjects, p. 70

a) The sly fox **b)** Several silly clowns **c)** Many different types of seashells **d)** The lights of the city **e)** A large black bear **f)** My friend Jessica **g)** Many children in my class **h)** The people of the town **i)** Fire trucks and firefighters

Complete Predicates, p. 71

a) swims in our pool every day **b)** ate all my mother's lilies **c)** tumbled out of the box **d)** made peanut butter sandwiches **e)** read newspapers only on weekends **f)** painted my bedroom mint green today **g)** contains multiplication problems **h)** rolled all the way down the hill

What Comes at the End of a Sentence? pp. 72–73

1. a) question mark **b)** exclamation mark or period **c)** exclamation mark **d)** question mark **e)** period **f)** exclamation mark or period **g)** question mark

2. Ensure that children have written the correct kind of sentence for each section.

One Sentence or Two? p. 74

a) I like Lisa. She is my friend. **b)** Paul likes to run. He runs fast. **c)** It was raining. I got wet. **d)** Dad told a story. It was funny. **e)** The telephone rang. It woke me up.

Joining Sentences with *And* or *But*, p. 75

1. a) but **b)** and **c)** but **d)** and

2. a) The sun is shining, **and** it is a nice day. **b)** Hans watered the plant, **but** it died. **c)** I wore a warm coat, **but** I was still cold. **d)** Jana likes reading, **and** she reads often. **e)** Dad found his glasses, **but** he lost them again.

Joining Sentences with *Or* or *So*, p. 76

1. a) or **b)** or **c)** so **d)** so **e)** or

2. a) Her bike had a flat tire, **so** she walked to school. **b)** I might keep this photo, **or** I might give it to Stanley. **c)** Sandra might keep her hair long, **or** she might get it cut short. **d)** Mika had dirty hands, **so** he washed them.

Sentences and Punctuation Review Quiz, pp. 77–78

1. a) Add an exclamation mark; strong feeling **b)** Add a period; telling **c)** Add a period OR exclamation mark; command **d)** Add a question mark; question **e)** Add a period; telling **f)** Add a question mark; question

2. a) Tina is funny. She makes me laugh. **b)** Correct **c)** The sun was shining. It was a nice day. **d)** The dogs are barking. They make lots of noise.

3. a) Alan plays piano, and he practices every day. **b)** I was tired, but I did not go to bed. **c)** Laura does not like grapes, but she ate two, anyway. **d)** The phone rang, and Dad answered it. **e)** Wayne looks sick, but he said he feels fine.

4. a) so **b)** or **c)** so **d)** so **e)** or

What Is a Contraction? p. 79

1. a) they're **b)** I'm **c)** We're **d)** you're **e)** It's **f)** that's

2. a) She's going to be upset if he's late. **b)** I'm sure that's my notebook.

More Contractions, p. 80

1. a) We'll **b)** you'll **c)** she'll **d)** I'll **e)** They'll **f)** he'll

2. a) I will bring sandwiches, and you will bring juice. We will have a great picnic!

Abbreviations, pp. 81–82

1. a) Dr. **b)** road **c)** St. **d)** avenue **e)** Dr., doctor **f)** Rd. **g)** street **h)** Ave.

2. a) Dr. Grayson went to school with Mrs. Scott. **b)** Wilson Ave. is near Westside Park. **c)** How close is Tower Rd. to where Mr. Castle works? **d)** Are there lots of trees on your street?

Contractions and Abbreviations Review Quiz, pp. 83–84

1. a) he's **b)** it's **c)** We'll **d)** I'll **e)** That's **f)** you'll **g)** They're

2. a) she will **b)** I am **c)** We are **d)** they will **e)** you are **f)** She is **g)** he will **h)** They will

3. a) Dr. **b)** Mr. **c)** Ave. **d)** Rd.

4. a) You're going to be taller than your father. **b)** Mrs. Henderson thinks that's a wonderful idea. **c)** He's certain that Alfonso lives on this street. **d)** They're walking their dog along Wilson Rd. **e)** Western Ave. is closed because it's flooded.

Using *To, Too,* or *Two*, p. 85

1. a) to **b)** too **c)** to **d)** too **e)** to **f)** too

2. a) to, two **b)** too, to, two **c)** two, to **d)** two, two, too

Write the Correct Word, p. 86

a) right **b)** sea **c)** right **d)** here **e)** write **f)** see **g)** hear **h)** right, right **i)** see, sea, here

Correcting Errors: "The Lost Mitten," p. 87

Paragraph 1, sentence 5: Where was <u>it</u>?

Paragraph 2, sentence 3: I looked in my <u>sister's</u> bedroom.

Paragraph 2, sentence 4: I looked in the kitchen and the living room, <u>too</u>.

Paragraph 3, sentence 1: I felt <u>sad. I</u> loved my blue mittens.

Paragraph 3, sentence 2: I had <u>two</u> other pairs of mittens, but the blue mittens were the <u>warmest</u>.

Paragraph 3, sentence 5: I always say goodbye to <u>Freddy</u> before I go to school.

Paragraph 4, sentence 2: Can you guess what I found under <u>Freddy's</u> paw?

© Chalkboard Publishing

Correcting Errors: "Owls," p. 88

Paragraph 1, sentence 2: An <u>owl's</u> feathers can be gray, brown, or white.

Paragraph 1, sentence 3: You can find owls in the United <u>States, Canada</u>, and many other countries around the world.

Paragraph 2, sentence 1: Have you ever seen an <u>owl?</u>

Paragraph 2, sentence 3: <u>That's</u> because owls sleep during the day.

Paragraph 3, sentence 1: Owls are good <u>hunters. They</u> can <u>hear</u> very soft sounds.

Paragraph 3, sentence 2: Owls have large eyes that can <u>see</u> at night, and they have strong, sharp claws, <u>too</u>.

Paragraph 3, sentence 3: Owls hunt frogs, <u>mice</u>, bugs, and birds.

Vocabulary List 1, pp. 89–90

a) convinced **b)** purpose **c)** resident **d)** recall **e)** ancient **f)** convince **g)** resident **h)** purpose **i)** recall **j)** ancient

Vocabulary List 1: Review, p. 91

1. a) purpose **b)** convince **c)** resident **d)** ancient **e)** recall

2. a) purpose **b)** recalled **c)** convinced **d)** resident **e)** convince **f)** ancient

Vocabulary List 2, pp. 92–93

a) signal **b)** observed **c)** vehicle **d)** annual **e)** predict **f)** signals **g)** vehicle **h)** predict **i)** signal **j)** observed **k)** annual

Vocabulary List 2: Review, p. 94

1. a) signal **b)** annual **c)** vehicle **d)** predict **e)** signal **f)** observe

2. a) predict **b)** vehicle **c)** annual **d)** signal **e)** observed **f)** signal

Vocabulary List 3, pp. 95–96

a) attempt **b)** rarely **c)** device **d)** actual **e)** prevent **f)** attempted **g)** rarely **h)** actual **i)** prevent **j)** device

Vocabulary List 3: Review, p. 97

1. a) attempt **b)** rarely **c)** prevent **d)** device **e)** actual **f)** attempt

2. a) prevent **b)** attempt **c)** device **d)** rarely **e)** actual

Vocabulary List 4, pp. 98–99

a) crumpled **b)** swift **c)** gradual **d)** clinging **e)** arranges **f)** brief **g)** swiftly **h)** clinging **i)** gradual **j)** brief **k)** arranged

Vocabulary List 4: Review, p. 100

1. a) gradual **b)** swift **c)** arrange **d)** cling **e)** crumple **f)** swift

2. a) brief **b)** gradual **c)** swift **d)** crumpled **e)** arranging **f)** swift

Vocabulary List 5, pp. 101–102

a) marsh **b)** risk **c)** clever **d)** avoid **e)** dozed **f)** fluttering **g)** marsh **h)** risk **i)** clever **j)** avoid **k)** dozed

Vocabulary List 5: Review, p. 103

1. a) fluttering **b)** avoid **c)** risk **d)** marsh **e)** doze **f)** clever **g)** risk

2. a) fluttered **b)** risk **c)** doze **d)** avoided **e)** clever **f)** risk **g)** marsh

© Chalkboard Publishing

1. **a)** dog, ball, park **b)** children, paintings, fingers **c)** uncle, hammer, nails, shed **d)** Kittens, puppies, pets, families, children **e)** Marco, soccer, baseball

2. **a)** bunches **b)** children **c)** puppies **d)** zeros **e)** foxes **f)** elves **g)** potatoes **h)** photos **i)** berries **j)** roofs

3. **a)** brothers' **b)** officer's **c)** hamsters' **d)** Sunday's

4. **a)** Karen hopes that <u>she</u> can go camping with <u>them</u> this summer. **b)** <u>We</u> are going to the zoo tomorrow with <u>her</u>. **c)** <u>They</u> played with <u>him</u>.

5. **a)** his **b)** her, its **c)** their

6. **a)** Hers is heavier than mine. **b)** Yours are more colorful than theirs. **c)** Their bell is as loud as its bell.

7. **a)** Circle "another" and underline "movie," draw an arrow from "another" to "movie"; circle "tired" and underline "everyone," draw an arrow from "tired" to "everyone." **b)** Circle "delicious" and underline "burgers," draw an arrow from "delicious" to "burgers." **c)** Circle "young" and underline "squirrels," draw an arrow from "young" to "squirrels"; circle "playful" and underline "squirrels," draw an arrow from "playful" to "squirrels." **d)** Circle "Bright" and underline "lightning," draw an arrow from "Bright" to "lightning"; circle "stormy" and underline "sky," draw an arrow from "stormy" to "sky."

8. **a)** the strongest **b)** taller **c)** the prettiest

9. **a)** more **b)** the most **c)** the most

10. **a)** A, a **b)** the, an **c)** an, a **d)** the, the

11. **a)** kicked, passed **b)** mixed, baked **c)** pulled, planted, watered **d)** Making, laughing

12. **a)** makes, **b)** mixes **c)** hatches

13. **a)** asked **b)** washed **c)** bought

14. **a)** will go **b)** will make **c)** will walk **d)** will stitch

15. **a)** underline "lost" and "found" **b)** circle "are" **c)** circle "is" **d)** underline "folded" and "tucked"

16. **a)** circle "are" and underline "going" **b)** circle "will" and underline "run" **c)** circle "is" and underline "excited" **d)** circle "is" and underline "hungry" and "drools"

17. **a)** run **b)** sweeps **c)** flashes **d)** flies **e)** rips

18. **a)** was **b)** had **c)** were **d)** were

19. **a)** always **b)** Tuesdays **c)** everywhere **d)** loudly **e)** rarely

20. **a)** exclamation mark, strong feeling **b)** period, telling **c)** question mark, question **d)** period, telling **e)** period, command

21. **a)** It's **b)** You'll **c)** I'm **d)** They're **e)** she's

© Chalkboard Publishing

www.ingramcontent.com/pod-product-compliance
Lightning Source LLC
Chambersburg PA
CBHW080324030726

47593CB00009B/2872